Blueprint for Local Harmony

A People's Guide to Utopia

Edmund Mazeika

Woke Mind Press: New Orleans, LA

Wise Animal Media d/b/a *Woke Mind Press*: New Orleans, Louisiana

All Bible Quotations: *New Jerusalem Bible*

No Artificial Intelligence was used in the writing of this book.

Cover done by Author with *Inkscape*

Internal formatting done by Author in *Atticus*

Self-Categorization: Romantic Philosophy

Formal categories [18]: philosophy, history, psychology, sociology, political science, economics, entrepreneurship, banking and finance, urban planning, architecture, agriculture, anthropology, archeology, education, religion, theology, geography, housing

Informal categories: futurism, civilization design, over-population crisis, urban renewal, rural renewal, bringing back the family farm, housing crisis,

I write my own promotional material because nobody knows my work better than I do, and even if my homespun marketing comes across a little rough at it least it doesn't read like a travel brochure you would pick up in a hotel lobby.

The name *Woke Mind Press* is inspired by Andrew Jackson's adoption of the pejorative jackass as the symbol of his new Democrat Party. Woke is such a great word with a great origin story.

The cover was inspired by *Future Shock* by Alvin Toffler: 1970. The subtitle was inspired by *The People's Guide to Mexico* by Carl Franz, one of my favorite books.

I.S.B.N. number: 979-8-9940708-0-2

contact@wokemindpress.com

Contents

One

THE QUEST FOR HARMONY

1.–The Human Mystery

F ar removed from the city lights and smog, strolling through a romantic meadow or pulled over on the side of a lonely country road; on clear evenings, people are drawn to gaze at the night sky displaying its full glory. Across the ceiling of the temple of the heavens, one beholds thousands of twinkling stars and planets intersected by the soft white bands of the Milky Way. Meteors pierce the darkness of the upper atmosphere flaring into falling stars. While admiring the endless cosmos, stargazers are inspired to contemplate the vastness of the Universe.

With even the weakest telescope, viewers can behold a dense tableau of celestial bodies. Powerful telescopes perched on mountaintops and orbiting in outer space peer ever deeper into galaxies far away. Rover robots explore the Martian landscape. Probes relay spectacular photographs of the moons of Jupiter and the rings of Saturn. Yet the stellar skies above have little to do with people's immediate or ultimate concerns. It is the human universe that impacts people. On our deep-blue, cloud-shrouded Planet Earth, humankind have come to depend on one another—for better and for worse. Although extraterrestrial enigmas abound, we must remain on Earth to solve the human mystery.

Before our planet was fully explored, mythical tales of paradises hidden in misty mountain valleys and on remote islands inspired adventurers to explore uncharted territories. After many failed attempts at ideal societies, there is a pervasive belief that a perfect society is not possible. Our media, entertainment and literature continually emphasize this point. Dramatists can't help but portray people as possessed with a fatal flaw that dooms humankind. Movie makers recognize the box-office draw of a dystopian future. I'd like to rewrite that apocalyptic script with a story of people who pioneer a bright future discovering the best possible way to live.

I have come to believe that the Utopia people are searching for is not a place to be discovered—it is a place that we can create. This book outlines a scheme for doing just that by establishing a radically superior economic, social and political organization that promotes harmony and prosperity by its participants organizing in a way that brings out the best in their human nature. We all want to have it all, to have our cake and eat it too and the way I will show you begins at the Gate of Goodness admonishing you that you cannot expect good unless you are good.

What better way to convince you utopia is possible than by giving you a complete set of instructions to build one? I characterize this book as *romantic philosophy* for we seek to accomplish the transcendent and do the impossible all in the service of the betterment of humankind. Seldom is heard a word discouraging thinking big or aiming high. If an ideal society is unattainable, then perhaps just aiming for perfection will produce something significantly better. You can characterize this book as a constructive fantasy offering up plenty of ideas for your personal vision: mental building blocks for your mind's playset. You can describe this book as a harsh critique of modern society expressed through the presentation of a comprehensive solution. This book does concentrate on small-city revival and creating prosperity in rural areas.

The ideas behind this book came to me during a two-year transcontinental hitchhiking odyssey. For me and many of my generation, exploring the country by traveling the open road was our vision quest. At the age of thirty-three, I left New York City to embark on an adventure to explore the United States. I wanted to visit the destinations I'd personally mythologized while studying the *National Geographic* maps I hung on my wall when I was growing up.

I had grown tired of hearing other travelers' Montana and California stories and was itching to hit the road to see for myself. During those years, I had the most fun for the least amount of money. I was in love with the open road and the journey forever ahead. Hitchhiking proved to be an inexpensive way to explore the country. Paradoxically, the financially poorest years of my life turned out to be some of the happiest and most inspiring.

During my travels, I visited many cities I had come to idealize because so many fellow travelers had praised them. I soon discovered that every city, no matter how large or small, scenic or exciting, suffered from the same problems of crime and poverty. I came to the conclusion that the root cause of most problems could be found in the basic economic, social and political organization of every community I'd encountered.

During my vagabond years, I happened to be going through a spiritual phase. Exploring churches, synagogues, mosques, ashrams and even a few cults was a great way to meet religious people and learn how they perceived the world and explained life's mysteries. I had a lot of memorable experiences and met plenty of well-meaning folks; but unfortunately, I did not find the answers I was looking for. My disappointment with organized religion, my study of economics and my experience starting several businesses inspired the vision that led to this book—the place I was looking for—where people lived in harmony—was actually in my imagination. My frustrations became a bountiful source of inspiration for improving the world.

Current events can be a real bummer. A disturbing documentary or a tragic news story can be upsetting, but reading an entire book detailing a critical social, economic or political issue can be highly unsettling. It is wise to be an informed citizen, but what purpose does it serve to learn the ins and outs of a pressing issue if we are powerless to do anything about it? This book considers forces within our control and gives us some ideas about what to do about the world's problems. This *People's Guide* puts you in the driver's seat with a roadmap by your side.

Throughout history, entrenched powers have hindered economic, social and political progress. Powerful people tend to persist in the questionable practices that grant them wealth and prestige. Even when presented with evidence proving what they are doing is harmful, detaching stubborn minds from the falsehoods they have come to believe is near impossible.

Let us strive to be wise animals by planting, growing and harvesting great ideas. What's the use of all the wise ideas humankind has gathered throughout the ages if wisdom does not prevail? Wild animals operate on instinct. Humans organize based on ideas, so it follows that the most successful organizations are based on the best ideas. Civilized human life thrives on cooperation, so the optimal way to organize is to the best way to cooperate.

We can do most anything if we are determined to succeed. People have proven their ability to put their minds together to *solve the mystery*, to *break the code*, to *discover the treasure*, to *do the impossible* once again. Humanity continues to excel with amazing breakthroughs in many fields. Bright minds are continually proposing creative solutions to every problem imaginable.

Some futurists believe perfecting artificial intelligence will be humanity's greatest achievement. Others insist colonizing Mars will eclipse all previous human accomplishments. I strongly beg to differ—Creating a harmonious, thriving society will be humankind's greatest triumph, because without that—everything else we have accomplished will be for naught.

2.–The New Promised Land

The 1970s were good times for growing up in New York. The City was a dynamic, bustling place with an enormous range of art, entertainment and culture. With all the progressive thinking in circulation, I was under the impression the world was becoming a better place. My mind was opened to pursuing great things and seeking knowledge wherever I could find it.

The garden apartment I grew up in had a small plot where my mother cultivated a variety of flowers. Toward the back of the garden, we buried our kitchen scraps and dining room leftovers. I was fascinated by how the colorful organic matter we buried in the ground rotted into rich brown soil in a little more than a month. At a tender age I became an avid composter. For most of the history of agriculture, farmers fertilized their soil by composting all sorts of organic matter. I was also fascinated by how scrap metal could be melted to be reused over and over again. At the dawn of metallurgy, people recycled all the metal they painstakingly mined by hand. Somehow, the prudent practices of composting and recycling have fallen out of favor.

During my youth, many exotic spiritual, medical and athletic practices came to America from foreign shores. Gurus espousing their variations of Hinduism sought fresh converts on American shores. Hippies adopted the Eastern beliefs of karma and reincarnation; and explored yoga and meditation. Music masters from India imported mystical music they made with exotic instruments. Ravi Shankar, the famous sitar player, played an annual concert at Carnegie Hall. Master martial artists from Japan, Korea and China imported judo, karate, tai-kwon-do and kung fu. Bruce Lee, the kung-fu fighter and actor made a high art of hand-to-hand combat and his tragic death at age thirty-two made him a hero for many young men who dreamed of being able to beat back the neighborhood bullies. Remote cloud-draped Far Eastern monasteries where masters trained their disciples in martial arts became ingrained in the ethos of my generation.

A wave of creative thinkers wrote books and gave lectures describing a great untapped human potential. It was popular to play with ideologies and experiment with new identities: to become a Buddhist, a vegetarian or the follower of an exotic guru. Young rebels were driven to be original. Our youthful conversations tended to disparage the adoption of traditional career paths. We were preoccupied with trans-forming ourselves through the exploration of new life paths.

Revolutions are messy affairs, and the hippies' brief heyday from the late 60s to the early 70s was no exception. Despite mixed results, their movement inspired many idealists to work toward a better future. Altruistic thinking tilled the fallow ground of many imaginations and planted optimistic ideas for a better future. Many assumptions and traditions were questioned, turned upside down, picked apart and put back together. I had many friends and teachers who were like-minded, freethinking, yearning for change and hoping for a better future.

At the age of sixteen, I read *The Limits to Growth*, a re-port presented by M.I.T. based on extensive research by the

Club of Rome, portending how non-renewable resources will become scarcer and more expensive if we squander the limited supply. With a finite quantity of a rather long list of nonrenewable mineral resources, it only makes sense to conserve and recycle whenever possible.

Most of the young people of my generation were anti-establishment. Many media outlets readily supplied information to inspire revolutionary minds. W.B.A.I.–99.5 FM was a vibrant alternative news source for our wayward generation. During my childhood, the Civil Rights Movement helped African Americans gain greater rights. The Women's Liberation Movement continued to open doors and break ceilings. It seemed like the United States was at the dawn of a great renaissance. I was led to believe I was going to live my adult life in the superior society spawned by this awakening.

Many years later, I am still perplexed by the way people behave in such counterproductive ways. One must wonder if love is what people want, what people celebrate, what people sing about, why is there still so much hatred in the world? If love is what people value above all else, why do so many people continue to tear one another apart when so much more can be accomplished when we build one another up? How can people emancipate themselves from vicious cycles of destructive behavior to move forward to a brighter future? It's about time people figured out how to live in harmony—how to love one another in a big way.

People are a puzzle. After encountering good people who go out of their way to help us out of a bind, we are left to wonder why everybody isn't like that. On the other hand, when we have the misfortune and displeasure of dealing with some decidedly bad people, we are left to wonder once again why there are so many difficult, devious, low-life, rotten people in the world. Where do they all come from? How did they get that way and why do they stay that way?

Most organizations operate for the benefit of a minority in power at the expense of the majority under their power. The way to get to the root of inequality is to organize in a way that first recognizes and then resolves inequalities. Throughout history, many seemingly impossible tasks have challenged the common imagination. Responding to insurmountable challenges, people have risen from obscurity, overcome the impossible and claimed their place in history. All along, skeptics insisted it couldn't be done until someone did it.

The perennial quest to improve people's quality of living inspired the inventions we couldn't dream of living without today. Many feats such as flight, space travel, organ transplants and instant transcontinental telecommunication were first believed to be impossible but are now taken for granted. What were first novelties are now commonplace. What were once luxuries are now necessities. Invention, discovery, research and the continual improvements they grant march on; yet the perennial problems of war, starvation, crime and poverty persist. It seems however positive the original concepts and intents of businesses and governments; conflict and disharmony arise as if *bad* was built into the process of organizing. What we have yet to invent is a way of organizing that does not bring out the *bad*—the demons in human nature.

Concerned people may ponder what they can do to live a life that has significance; how they can make a difference. They wonder if anyone can find true peace by accepting this crazy world. Restless spirits long for transformation. Self-help literature can be insightful, yet changing oneself by oneself can only go so far. Gurus promise personal transformation—for a price. Urbanites pay good money to attend weekend retreats in search of some enlightenment or self-realization. After a few massage treatments, group meditations and power seminars, they may come home a little refreshed and uplifted; but once the buzz wears off, little has changed. Seekers resume the same frustrated lives they were living before, only with a few hundred (or thousand) dollars less in their bank accounts. Oh well.

Many misfortunate people are given little choice but to leave their homes. They flee natural disasters, poverty, gang violence and oppression. Wary emigrants cross borders to overcome barriers of culture and language to start anew. City folk move to the country to pursue a simpler life. Country folk move to the city to pursue greater opportunity. Some find what they are looking for. Most continue to search. Where is the next horizon? What lies beyond it? Where is the Promised Land now?

The next horizon is a land, a people, a community living in loving harmony. The Promised Land is underneath your feet: the beautiful Planet Earth. The goal of pursuing local harmony is crystal clear: to create an open and egalitarian society where every member can thrive. By working to live in loving harmony, determined people will discover the greatest satisfaction in living and the profoundest purpose in dying. Striving for a life without conflict is so simple a child can understand it. Embracing conflict is so complicated no adult can fully explain or justify it.

The vast past lies behind—the future lies ahead. We have a choice. It is not a matter of should-or-shouldn't or right-or-wrong. Establishing an enlightened society can be accomplished by people settling their squabbles and integrating their efforts. Finding a way to get along is so fundamental, it's worth the time and sacrifice we will need to give it. Before we all blow each other up, let us consider every possible way to get past the negative to move toward the positive.

The answer, my friends, is no longer blowing in the wind—the answer is local harmony, today and forever. The challenging endeavor of establishing a truly harmonious society will give our lives a clear direction, a real meaning and a greater purpose. We will transform ourselves by transforming the world together. Life's great mysteries are perplexing yet discovering a way to love one another in a big way will begin to solve the human mystery.

3.–Human Revolution

After my hitchhiking adventure, I decided to go into the building trades as a carpenter. At the start, I was enchanted by this romantic change in careers; after all, carpenters who master their profession are called journeymen. Once I had learned my trade, I would be able to travel to exotic destinations and work wherever I wanted. However, after a few months, I became dismayed by the role reversal I had chosen. I went from being the leader of my own organizations to a follower in other people's organizations. I was surprised by the way I was treated and disenchanted with the pervasive bad leadership and poor communication.

The way I saw it, the work culture of the building trades was backward. I'd always treated the people who worked for me well and they loved me for it, so I came to the conclusion that the mean bosses who pushed me around had it all wrong. By making me miserable they were unintentionally making themselves miserable. I put up with a lot of unenlightened leadership to learn my trade. My frustrating experiences working in construction inspired me to espouse an open business culture that promotes full communication and mutual respect.

Establishing a superior society or starting a better business is a complicated affair; yet at its roots, it begins with the simple concept of people treating one another well. The basic idea behind the sophisticated notion of enlightenment is people improving the way they treat one another. The driving force behind every rebellion and revolution is the people's desire to be treated better and given their fair share. And since both the oppressed and the oppressor are miserable as a result, emancipating people from oppressing one another is the only way for everyone to truly live better lives.

More than two centuries ago, the European Enlightenment inspired England's Glorious Revolution of 1688, the American Revolution in 1776 and the French Revolution in 1789. From these transformations, the first modern democracies arose in Europe and America. Shortly afterward, the development of efficient steam engines fostered the start of the Industrial Revolution. Not too long after that, they set steam engines to drive steel wheels, and the rapid adoption of railroad technology across the world sparked a Transportation Revolution. A century and a half later, advances in rocket technology spawned a spectacular Aeronautics Revolution. A few decades after that, progress in computer technology gave birth to the Information Technology Revolution.

Despite so many revolutions spawning so much miraculous technology, the prospects for humankind remain dim. Instead of coming together, many forces continue to drive humanity apart. The next revolution must be the greatest revolution of them all—the Human Revolution—when our species finally learns to get along in a big way. The moment people try to control one another is the moment the fun ends. The moment people treat one another as equals is the moment the fun begins. Across the world, despite a multitude of cultural differences, most people's guiding values and individual aspirations are not as different as they may appear. Most people value more or less the same things: liberty, respect, compelling entertainment, challenging recreation, good food, friends and family. Every human being on Earth wants to live a good life, have fun and be happy. By liberating themselves from oppressing one another, the people give themselves the gift of true freedom.

Altruism is extremely rare in the Animal Kingdom. Adventurous people wandering into the tropical wilderness are well-advised to keep their eyes and ears open while exploring the jungle—hidden predators lie in wait ready to ambush their next victim. Unfortunately, predation persists in the civilized world as well. Modern societies can be likened to jungles or shark-infested waters, but it doesn't have to be that way. The key to creating a better society is to escape the jungle and forsake the shark-infested waters by pioneering social and political systems that are vital because they are altruistic.

Many people have experienced what I call a "Woodstock feeling" of purposeful togetherness. Attending a ballgame, crowd waves undulate around the stadium; the people cheer and for a few brief moments, fans feel part of a greater whole. Later that evening, they each return home to their separate lives. When people feel upset, it's good to see their friends. Banter and laughter distract us from our problems, so we feel a little better; yet after the party's over, pressing concerns resurface. Ambitious people might have a lot on their mind, but without someone to share the load, they often fail to resolve their difficulties. It can be stressful to be one's own life coach, personal assistant, business manager and workforce. The people can better solve their problems and achieve their goals by supporting one another and unifying their efforts, so it's high time for people longing for real progress to join forces.

Let us start a society afresh without letting any spoilers join our game. The first challenge is keeping rotten people out. Hurting others is easy for rotten people. They hurl their weapons without forethought. Hurting can take an instant—healing can take a lifetime. Peace-seeking pioneers emancipate themselves from negativity—famous for breeding more negativity—to move toward sustained positivity. Negativity is nothing but a drain. Hard-hearted people who are experts at putting people down and pushing them around can stay on their side of town.

The secret formula for fully harnessing the human potential and establishing harmony is the Golden Rule. When everybody treats everyone else how they want to be treated, they give themselves the gift of greater freedom and peace of mind. Emancipated from constant conflict, we can advance to ever-higher levels of knowledge and creativity rather than being distracted by the latest hassles, mishaps and misunderstandings. When the people put their highest values into practice in all spheres of activity to form enlightened societies, their social evolution will catch up with humankind's technological evolution. The people will challenge each other, motivate one another—even push one another—to do their utmost to succeed. They will encourage the survival of every liberating idea while working toward the extinction of every limiting idea.

Economic progress is hindered when powerful people rig the economic and political system in their favor. The key that unlocks the door to prosperity for all is establishing a system incapable of being rigged in which the stakeholders share their fortunes *and misfortunes*. In a fair-minded society, people enjoy the tranquility of dealing day-to-day with honest and reliable people. What could be better than that? Yet—it can get better than that.

A group of fair-minded people organized for their mutual

benefit can harness the power of their fairness toward peace and prosperity by establishing their very own enterprise system. Their honesty, trust and goodwill can be counted as economic assets. Such a fresh system of enlightened entrepreneurship that prioritizes people over profits resolves the greatest challenge in human relations—discovering a way to create wealth that draws a society together rather than segregating it into impervious classes.

Many struggling people are feeling angry at the world. They are certainly not alone. However, attempting to resolve issues by hastily acting out of anger is ill-advised. Many regrettable deeds have been done in the heat of the moment. People possessed by anger need to chill out and get their head straight by considering the possible consequences of any rash actions. Revenge does not yield lasting satisfaction. It is wiser to channel anger toward solving problems rather than settling scores. Revenge is the link in the chain of action that keeps wickedness alive. Revenge is a natural response, yet angry feelings depress the spirit, and ill deeds chain their doers to the cycle of evil. Anger only looks backward. Love looks forward. Anger distorts understanding. Love clarifies understanding. Forsaking revenge frees the mind, raises the spirit and liberates people from being slaves to a dark past and inspires them to become creators of a bright future.

We often feel stuck in a rut. Life relentlessly repeats itself with the same monotonous routine: day-in, day-out;

week-in, week-out; month-after-month; year-after-year. The disenchanted long for something more out of life. Maybe it's time to hit the road. Fortune often does favor the bold and many restless people will discover greater happiness pursuing meaningful and challenging ventures that reactivate their lives. A passionate pursuit of harmony can fulfill a spiritual quest to discover meaning and purpose—to live a life without compromise—to live a life without dismissing the plight of others less fortunate in order to gain a meaningless fortune—to succeed by opening our hearts.

Enlightened organizations will be liberated from the self-perpetuating cycles of conquer, subjugation and rebellion. Harmonious societies will generate never-ending cycles of cooperation, integration, high-vibration and better communication supporting dynamic and peaceful lives—such is a true Human Revolution. If *success* is being able to thrive in one's environment, then the ultimate human environment is one in which everyone thrives. It's about time for the people to stop crying, stop lying—stop defying one another and switch to the better way of harmonious living so close at hand.

Establishing an enlightened society begins and ends with how people relate to one another, and there's nothing very cosmic about that. How to cultivate the best in our human nature is no profound mystery—I treat you well, you treat me well; everyone treats one another well and we all go better places from there. The challenge is how to organize human affairs so kindness and courtesy are practiced consistently enough for harmony to grow. Harmony can prevail when we concentrate on cultivating our strengths rather than preying on weaknesses. The selfish pursuit of wealth has surely proven its power to bring out the devil in people. The fresh way of organizing described in the pages ahead will bring out the better angels of our human nature... finally.

4.–Entrepreneurial Revolution

My introduction to entrepreneurship was on the pearly white sands of the vast, roaring Atlantic coast of North America selling jewelry on the beach. It was much nicer working barefoot in the sand than in a stuffy office in downtown Manhattan as I had for most of the previous two years. I spent my days dealing with young women wearing bikinis rather than uptight administrators in pinstripe suits. Shell necklaces hung from my right arm, and I carried a folded, black-velvet display-board of attractive handmade earrings propped up in my left hand. I would walk up to people lounging on their beach blankets and politely ask, "Can I show you some beautiful jewelry?" On real busy days, I would hardly have to solicit; people would call me over from blanket to blanket.

Ankle bracelets proved especially popular. My mother, a

veteran freelance artist, showed an interest in designing and making anklets. We soon figured out how to string up beads, and right there on the dining-room table, she began producing original beaded jewelry. Before long we acquired quite a bead collection: shell beads from the Philippines, glass beads from Czechoslovakia and exotic wooden beads from Africa. Egg cartons made a great way to organize the bead collection. Our ankle-bracelet-production facility in the family dining room was my introduction to cottage industry.

My mother and I dreamed beyond the beach and the fabulous one-hundred-day summer season. We plotted other ways of retailing and wholesaling our homespun creations. After fourteen years as a batik artist, my mother discovered the artistic possibilities of beading and fell in love with a new art. Soon she was earning a living making jewelry. Over the next few years, several people who got their start working with me would go on to earn a living in the costume jewelry business.

Sporting shoulder-length blond hair, many beach goers assumed I was a surfer from California. People called me "Puka Man" after the shells found in Hawaii even though I was selling shell jewelry imported from Asia. I explored new shorelines farther east and discovered more beaches where I could ply my trade. I brought some buddies to the beach, set them up with merchandise and took my cut. My income increased significantly with my first associate salespeople. A few summers later I had hired more than a dozen people to sell my jewelry across three counties from Rockaway Beach to West Hampton. Several people who worked with me were inspired to start their own businesses. This led me to believe there are plenty of people who would go into business for themselves if they had the support to make the leap.

Instead of ineffectively demonstrating against the establishment, entrepreneurial activists can demonstrate superior ways of producing goods and providing services. People longing for change can exchange their hopes for reality through entrepreneurship. When honest businesses supplant dishonest ones, people can begin to solve many of the fundamental problems plaguing our societies. Safe, clean, fair businesses can be islands of harmony in a dangerous, dirty and unfair world. A local network of businesses working together without exploiting people or harming the natural environment will be able to establish a haven of harmony.

Some people have too much, most have too little and fewer still are truly happy. Wherever you go, people are still singing the same worn-out, old tunes. Poor people lament their poverty. Wealthy people are baffled by the luxuries that fail to give them the happiness they felt was their due. The human race needs a better way of doing business. It's about time for a change. All too often, employees are mere marionettes on a stage controlled by puppet masters above. Employees are the ones who suffer from mismanagement and corruption at the top.

Clicking through the pages of a big-city commercial directory, one is drawn to ponder the countless organizations doing business in that city. Large cities are sustained by a dizzying array of organizations—tiny, small, medium and large businesses and institutions. These collections of organizations, unequal in power and position, both cooperating and struggling against one another, create the marvel and the mess of competition in the modern world. Enlightened entrepreneurs aim for a future with more marvels and less mess.

In a greedy, deceitful, money-hungry business world, integrity is uncommon, yet cultivating a good working spirit is no great mystery. Work is work—there's no way of getting around work. Yet working in an open and supportive fellowship is always more fun and satisfying. Many businesses begin with high ideals, yet they compromise their values to stay in business. Businesses in highly competitive industries are motivated to adopt the same crooked practices (shortcuts, cover-ups, gimmicks, little white lies, etc.) their competitors use. Enlightened entrepreneurs build on a solid base of sound principles rather than compromising. They maintain their unbending integrity and stalwart adherence to high values as the very cornerstone of their enterprise, so their hearts are open, their minds are free, they can take pride in what they do, and they have nothing to hide.

High-minded community leaders are hard at work doing their best to improve their neighbors' lives. Such efforts should be honored and applauded, yet most community activists are fighting an uphill battle. The average citizen says, "That's the way it's been since I can remember, so how can it change now?" Persistent economic, social and political problems are so entrenched, many consider them to be natural features of the landscape. Substandard education, a poor work ethic and political corruption are so pervasive they are nearly impossible to root out completely from established societies. The good news is it can change now.

Most working people earn a wholesale wage, then pay retail for most of what they buy. Their employer profits from their work. The people they do business with profit from their purchases. Both their wages and their purchases are taxed. After all their hard work and the hassles they must endure, many people find it difficult to balance their budget so they can live within their means.

The people at the top of successful businesses earn tens, hundreds, even thousands of times more than the people at the bottom. The pursuit of the highest possible shareholder value and executive compensation inspires the exploitation of people and the natural environment to maximize profits. In order to justify production practices harmful to the environment, creative public-relations departments spend good money to project an environmentally friendly "green" image that belies their company's real motives and practices. Special interests lavishly fund "think tanks" to promote counterfeit science and espouse exotic philosophies. From castles in the sky, business leaders remotely control the empires they reign over. Company leaders far removed from their factories often don't know any of the workers and may have never even visited their town. Without so much as an employee survey, corporate executives have derailed thousands of lives with plant shutdowns and worker layoffs.

There are two ways for striving people to succeed: either they placate the whims of the gatekeepers who control the keys to their success, or they start a new game played on their own gameboard. To succeed, you either have to jump through someone else's hoops or start your own circus. It's time for people longing for peaceful prosperity to take the plunge and go into business for themselves by establishing a revolutionary business culture based on full cooperation—not remote control—to establish businesses run by human beings for human beings. Businesses modern in the products and services they offer, yet old-fashioned by prioritizing people over profits.

Money represents energy. Money made fairly is clean energy. Guiding that clean energy through the right channels can lead to lasting success in many endeavors. It may seem an unconventional path to harmony and enlightenment—to

make and manage money well—yet it is *only* through enlightened businesses and honest money managers that the
world can be transformed. The only way to get ahead in
the real world is to beat the money grubbers at their own
game. Every business is an expression of the philosophy that
drives it. A business must earn a profit to thrive, yet money
need not be an end, rather the means to the higher goal of
local harmony and prosperity. Enlightened rebels fight for
change—but instead of trying to change how other people do business, entrepreneurial activists concentrate on the
challenges of their own enterprises. They mind their own
businesses rather than meddling in the affairs of others.

I remember many movies depicting good ol' boys gathered at the local country club; city commissioners running
their town from smoke-filled banquet rooms: crooked people gathered on colorful plantation-house verandas to drink
mint juleps and settle their scores. No one denies there is
significant corruption in business and government throughout much of the world. The pertinent questions concern
where the corruption lies hidden, who precisely is corrupt,
and how they get away with their chicanery. Every side claims
the others are up to no good. This book does not concern
itself with corruption in the greater world. This is a guide for
us to tap into the power of our goodness by abiding by high
principles from the start.

5.–Household Revolution

For the fourth summer I sold jewelry on the beach, I rented a five-bedroom house on Long Island in Nassau County. More than a dozen hippies came to live under my roof to sell my unique line of jewelry on all the major, and a few minor, beaches on the Island. This was the early peak of my empire. I had taken charge, gotten things organized and properly ascended to my rightful throne. I was the undisputed Jewelry King of Long Island commanding a small army that eventually made a few sales every place people congregated where sand and water met on the South Shore.

Our home base was Robert Moses State Park in western Suffolk County. I claimed Field Two westside: the spoiled brat, rich kid, party beach, where it was okay to blast your radio. Ellen and Brian, friends from Key West, came up for the summer. Jack parked his school bus in the driveway. Some people stayed for the entire season, while others came from all over the country to work the beaches for a few weeks. My buddy Terry came from Chicago and directed the movie for a week so I could attend the National Rainbow Gathering in western Pennsylvania. It turned out to be a great season. We later referred to it as the Magic Summer.

I fondly recall that summer because everyone in our humble household got along so well. Money wasn't an issue;

everyone made good money and had fun making it. Aside from one couple who had a few heated arguments, there was no drama. I was the dream boss—free and easy. If someone had walked in on us hanging out, they would have had a hard time guessing I was the mastermind of the operation. We had a big backyard with a volleyball net and a barbeque pit. We had such a happening scene; cool people came from all over to kick it at our pad.

No one in our household ever argued about money—we had enough. Everyone could afford to go to the movies or out on the town whenever they wanted. If you needed a ride, there was always someone headed your way. We had peace and prosperity. We had unintentionally created our own little village and returned to the way people were meant to live. From that experience, I came to the conclusion that when people enjoy their work, earn good money and a have comfortable home, living together in harmony is totally possible.

Nowadays, few people live as they did at the dawn of settled society in the primitive simplicity of a remote village nestled deep in the wilderness. Most people live in the complexity of the civilized world in a house or apartment. Despite living physically on top of each other, many residents are estranged from most of the people living around them. Neighbors nod their heads as they pass each other by on their way to wherever they are rushing to. "Latchkey kids" return from school to an empty home. Single folk come home to a vacant abode. Commuters hurry home from a hard day at work to fix dinner, unwind and watch some TV so most neighbors are too worn out to share time after work.

To "divide and conquer" is a war strategy widely expressed in everyday parlance. People are divided by fear, ill will and misinformation; then conquered by depression, addiction and loneliness. One of the principal ways to come together described in this book is people designing and developing their own neighborhoods as modern villages; herein called *private-commonwealth estates*. Residents of these intentional neighborhoods will enjoy their private lives; yet when they're in the mood for company they will be able to enjoy a rich social life with good neighbors.

Until quite recently it was common for extended families to live together. It must have been a lot of fun sharing a home with grandparents, uncles, aunts, and children of all ages fussing and fighting in one big household. 'Individual preferences and opportunities fostered by education drew family members in separate directions. Children went away to college and moved near and far to pursue professional careers. The more adventurous offspring discovered their lands of enchantment and settled in other parts of the country. The less adventurous ones moved to a part of town they preferred or could afford. Family resentments are famous for running long and deep. Grudges can last for decades.

Many disheartened people long for more of that "family feeling" because their families aren't giving them much of it anymore.

Ideally, people would choose to live together in harmony. Fortunately, there are many practical advantages that make living together realistically possible. There is safety in numbers. There is savings in numbers. It takes a village to raise a child, yet it also takes a village to properly care for older folks. By spending constructive time with their elders after school, children stay out of trouble. In their village homes, youngsters learn useful craft skills and play productive games rather than spending too much time looking at memes or on social media. When parents are not able to give proper attention to their rambunctious children, there will always be someone around to look after them. Instead of procrastinating over getting a leaky faucet repaired, residents can call on the estate handyman who can fix it in a couple of minutes. Instead of workshops sitting idle, with an adult to supervise them, children can get creative and stay productive while learning arts and crafts and making cool stuff.

In a private-commonwealth estate, each member's private residence may be spacious and well-appointed, yet their homes will not serve as status symbols. The wealth residents share in common will proclaim their mutual prosperity. Some may wonder if this is too much to ask. Many people are attached to the idea of being Lord of their manor or

Queen of their castle. Yet people who recognize the manifold advantages of egalitarian living let go of such silly notions. They share their wealth to get more from their wealth. The people rule together rather than ruling over one another.

Neighborhood cooperation reduces the cost of living. Cooking, eating and cleaning up together is less expensive and time consuming than eating alone. Buying food in bulk saves money and shopping time. Cooking for more people doesn't take that much more time. When people eat together, they are generally more relaxed; so they eat slower, chew more and digest better than eating on the run. The children learn valuable kitchen skills, develop proper table manners and cultivate a taste for healthier foods. Dinnertime once again becomes a forum for lively discussions. After mealtime, cleaning up and doing the dishes together lightens the burden of household chores.

Lively villages foster a rich social environment for people of all ages. Animated conversations between young and old help older folk stay up to date and inspire youngsters to cultivate greater patience and humility. Young people will glean valuable insights from their elders' wisecracking and war stories, and older folk will enjoy sharing their hard-won knowledge and perspective before those nuggets of wisdom are gone forever.

All too often, private interests own the best properties in town and public property is neglected. Sprawling factories and imposing wharfs block urban waterfronts. Pothole-ridden streets make cycling a drag and roller-skating nearly impossible. Weekend hobbyists use their workshops only occasionally. Many backyard swimming pools are used by the kids for only a couple of hours a week. Unsold and foreclosed properties stand idle. Many front yards and backyards are rarely used. Most apartment-building roofs are off limits to residents because of liability concerns. Private-commonwealth estates will put all useable space to good use.

The members of private-commonwealth estates will periodically gather to discuss local affairs in a Village Council. Members set up a circle of folding chairs to sit down to discuss the business of their village. There's a lot of things that need to be done to run a household for one hundred people plus guests. Who's going to mow the lawn? Who's in charge of the gardening this week? The youngest to the oldest will be invited to participate. Village Councils are the foundation of the larger governing system. Each estate will eventually appoint a representative to attend the general meeting.

An estate should keep a journal from its inception. Dates, times, incidents, the people who come and go fade from memory so quickly it is prudent to record them in a chronicle of local affairs. Inspired journalists will be called upon to sum things up and explain what's going on in their neighborhood in its historical context. Since everyone and his little brother has a cell phone with a camera, collecting and archiving the best photos of the day is a fun task that will enrich the chronicle. Time goes by, memories fade, people change and nothing turns out the way anyone thought it would, so your memory bank will only get more valuable over time. Before long, local historians will come snooping around asking for a look so they can take a deep dive into very local history.

6.–Economic Revolution

In my early twenties, I worked for the Federal Reserve on Liberty Street in downtown Manhattan. The New York Federal Reserve Bank is a fourteen-story, castle-like building featured in several movies, most notably *Die Hard 3*. When it was complete in 1924, it towered above the surrounding buildings while today it is overshadowed by the glass-and-steel skyscrapers looming over it. The famous basement vaults full of gold bullion descend five stories below street level. I worked in the funds-transfer department on the ground floor.

My humble job was to execute bank-to-bank money transfers over the phone for the smaller banks that did not have computerized electronic-transfer systems in place. Clerks were supplied with a list of code words to secure the transactions. It was a fun job because I enjoyed blabbing on the phone with the mostly female secretaries working somewhere in Upstate New York or on the Island. I would type out the transfer slips on an I.B.M. Selectric typewriter. Each slip was carbon copied in triplicate: white, yellow and pink. After I finished talking and typing, I placed the paperwork in the document conveyer belt beside my desk, which whisked it into the next room.

During my afternoon breaks, the fancy marble-and-brass trimmed elevators would take me to the 13th and 14th floor, which to my surprise were virtually abandoned. My exploration of the upper floors of this world banking capitol was on a strictly don't-ask–don't-tell basis. There were quite a few rooms to explore. The one that stood out was an elegant conference room with mahogany trimmed walls, paintings and burgundy leather couches on which I would occasionally sneak an afternoon nap. That conference room must have been where the big guys met to do all their fancy economic stuff. On clear days, I would sit in the castle turret on the 14th floor overlooking Maiden Lane. Framed between skyscrapers I enjoyed a narrow view of the East River and Brooklyn on the horizon.

When a major bank's computer system went down, the staff had to stay late. On one such evening, I transferred $1.3 billion from the Bank of New York to Chase Manhattan Bank. Transfers were limited to $99 million so I had to execute fourteen separate transfers. It's a shame I didn't earn a commission. One of the Fed's jobs is to manage the money supply by incinerating worn bank notes and replacing them with new ones. I cashed my paycheck at the pay window of the Money Room on the 9th floor. Behind the bullet-proof glass, forklifts carrying pallets of fresh cash traversed the cavernous room. I had the privilege of visiting the center of money distribution in New York City: the very Belly of the Beast. The cashier handed me my measly wages while $40,000,000 in fresh cash drove by behind him. An additional $200,000,000 in cash was stacked across the back of the room.

I didn't see much of a future working in the steel and concrete jungle like my father had for so many years. I had taken advantage of the savings plan, so when I tendered my resignation, I had a little money tucked away. During my college years, I had taken classes in macro- and micro-economics. That academic introduction to economics combined with my experience working at the Fed granted me a particular insight into the science of economics. In the more than forty years since then, the economy has become a more prominent topic in public discourse. Few people deny the importance of good economic policy.

People earn money, spend money, borrow money and lend money. Whenever and wherever people come together to buy and sell, they create a market. Markets are like organisms: they're born, they grow, they get sick and when not properly cared for they die. Economists are akin to market doctors. Markets can be unpredictable, yet economists do their best to forecast their behavior, nurture their growth and remedy any maladies.

Money is a medium of exchange and a store of value. People's toil, struggles and creativity are translated into money; so, in many ways, money represents life. Money is a tool that facilitates trade. Imagine publishing a book, building a house or putting on a concert if you could only barter. Like most tools, money can also be used for nefarious purposes. Some declare money is the root of all evil. Then others correct them by clarifying that it's the love of money. Deceiving others to gain more than one's fair share of money is the primary mode of evil. To express it most accurately, inequality is the root of most evil.

Human eyes tend to focus on the shiny, the bright and the healthy; yet beyond the outskirts of prosperity, multitudes live in squalor, destitution and homelessness. Millions of lives are marginalized by poverty. One shortcoming leads to another, perpetuating cycles of poverty and ensnaring people in its trap. Powerful business organizations lobby for tax cuts while public infrastructure is neglected and public services are chronically underfunded. As long as those in power can get away with the dirty games they play to stay at the top, people will be fighting back in response to their oppression. As long as there are bums and billionaires, there will be turmoil. Despite monumental efforts over many decades, most social systems woefully fail to emancipate any significant number of people from the clutches of poverty. Raising people out of poverty is an essential part of a genuine economic and social revolution; so, in this scheme, special attention is paid to the bottom rung of the Ladder to Success.

What is the recipe for prosperity for all? What is the main ingredient? Our recipe for a local economic revolution is to establish enlightened businesses that share their knowledge and resources to rapidly progress by learning and earning our way to a better life. The main ingredient is goodness: using wealth and knowledge to help people rather than harm them: investing surplus wealth to help the less fortunate so everyone progresses together.

Enlightened societies aspire to waste as little time and as few resources as possible. They strive to transact only good: good goods, good information, goodwill and good spirits for good times today and better days tomorrow. When a local economy is a wholly goodness-transacting system, the people will continually generate goodwill and generosity. These goodwill-generosity-generating systems of exchange will become the beating hearts of prosperous economies sustaining harmonious societies.

Over the course of history, generations of enterprising people have experimented with various methods of coordinating their efforts to prosper. Most organizations dedicate a significant portion of their wealth to collective efforts. The wealth accumulated by these collective efforts can be defined as a commonwealth. A commonwealth is literally a pooling of wealth collected for the mutual benefit of those who contribute to the pool. Households, clubs, businesses, tribes and governments can be characterized as commonwealths. Fifty-three former British colonies, first known as the British Commonwealth, are now referred to as the Commonwealth of Nations. Virginia, Kentucky, Massachusetts and Pennsylvania retain the title of commonwealth. In the broadest sense, any organization managing the collection and use of wealth is a commonwealth.

The term *commonwealth* is adopted herein for its plain-spoken accuracy, not to imply or connote anything. The term *private commonwealth* is used to identify four model organizations outlined in this plan. They are firms, households and the two types of amalgamations they form. Private commonwealths are limited in scale. *Private-commonwealth companies*, limited to ten principal members, develop a wide spectrum of businesses. Private-commonwealth estates, limited to one hundred residents, develop a variety of rich home environments. Companies and estates are amalgamated into a *people's corporation* limited to 10,000 members.

A people's corporation is an egalitarian institution owned by its shareholders. It is a democratic corporation established for the benefit of all of its members, not a dictatorial organization dedicated to maximizing the profits of a small group of shareholders. A people's corporation established in a remote location forms a *private-commonwealth municipality*—a private city-state—a sovereign, highly economically self-sufficient and politically autonomous realm.

An ideal location for a people's corporation is a small city (population 5,000 to 30,000). Small cities have a lower cost of living. Most small cities offer a wide range of developmental possibilities not available in big cities. In big metro areas, the price of real estate is significantly higher, agricultural opportunities are limited and the countryside beyond the suburbs is out of practical commuting range. Members of a successful people's corporation centered in a small city will be able to enjoy high-quality urban, suburban and rural living. In the urban core, dynamic living environments can be made in remodeled hotels, schools and factory buildings. Suburban estates could host businesses, schools and recreational facilities. Beyond the suburbs, residents will be able to enjoy many flavors of country living in a series of rural-estate retreats spread throughout the surrounding countryside.

Private commonwealths are run on a system of management-by-discussion. Shareholders discuss each issue for as long or as short as it takes to reach agreement. Consensus decision making is cooperative management motivated by members' mutual desire to figure out what will work best for everyone involved. The surest way to discover the best solution to any problem is to thoroughly research and discuss every option available. An analogous example in America is trial by jury. After discussing their impressions and interpretations, jurors are instructed to unanimously decide on a guilty or not-guilty verdict. The great 1958 film *Twelve Angry Men* produced by and starring Henry Fonda is a thorough exposition of the challenges, the hassles and the wisdom of the consensus process. In the movie, a hot-headed set of sequestered jurors is eager to convict, yet cooler heads prevail and a level-headed re-examination of the evidence leads to a not-guilty verdict.

Traditional property speculators invest money in land they believe will rise in value. Selling real estate to the highest bidder drives up rents, property taxes and the cost of living. Speculative bidding frenzies famously lead to irrational enthusiasm which unreasonably inflates prices blowing into bubbles that eventually burst. People's corporations will not bid up the price of their real estate to drive up their cost of living.

Calling all economists—! Let's establish a recession-proof local economy. When an amalgamated system of companies is able to satisfy unexpected demands during a downturn, their highly diversified business system will be able to significantly outperform the regional and national economy. A diverse network of businesses with ample productive resources, a large knowledge bank and a deep talent pool will be able to produce a wide and diverse range of goods and services. Diversified local economies are far more resilient than farm or factory economies. Droughts, poor trade policies and drops in commodity prices harm farm economies. Slowdowns and closures hurt poorly diversified factory towns.

Calling all entrepreneurs–! Let's establish a business system with built-in job security. By providing continuous job-related training, everyone's skills can stay ahead of the advancing technology so no one's job is outsourced. By developing skills in more than one vocation, workers will always have an alternative career path if one of those paths fizzles out.

Big economies are like wild, untamable lions—raging beasts that rarely behave correctly and can barely be subdued when they get out of control: Careful–! These small, local, centrally managed economies of the future will be like a cat purring on your lap.

7.–Social Revolution

Despite centuries of social and political progress since the European Enlightenment, inequality still pervades modern civilization. The imbalanced society is perpetuated by its double standards. There's one set of rules for *us*, and another set of rules for *them*. The double standards between the rich and the poor, between the powerful and the weak, have been thousands of years in the making. In slave societies, there's an absolute double standard between masters and slaves. Prisons run an iron oligarchy. The warden, staff and guards have complete control. Hierarchies put a few people in charge of many, alienating people from one another. Class societies segregate people by social status, ability and education into lower, middle and upper classes.

The lower-class struggle to get ahead and upper-class efforts to stay ahead inspire devious behavior. As a result of the perpetual struggle between the haves and the have-nots, a split way of thinking has developed in both groups. Two sets of conflicting values govern most human behavior—a higher set of family values that encourages loving, caring and sharing and—a lower set of transactional values that disregards the well-being of other people to accomplish selfish pursuits. If operating by a *double standard* is the problem, observing a *single standard* of conduct is the solution. Hard as one may try, faithfully following two rule books is confusing and burdensome because it is impossible to truly abide by conflicting sets of principles.

Establishing an enlightened society begins when the people fully share their advantages and fairly earn their prestige to form a true meritocracy. Equal access to education does not lead to equal outcomes, yet meritocracies strive for the fullest realization of the total human potential. While many people may be content satisfying their immediate wants by the most immediate means, the more ambitious members can distinguish themselves by achieving significantly more through dedicated learning and practice. Successful artists, academics and athletes will be able to enjoy the rewards of their distinctions without marginalizing their less ambitious or less talented colleagues.

An egalitarian fellowship is founded on a social contract of reciprocity that harmonizes the interests of all members. Such a fellowship can build a house forever united by openness and equality—never to be divided by an imbalance of power. When someone falls—others will be there to help them up. When champions claim victory—the people will cheer them on. Like big healthy families, the people will take care of one another. With a strong commitment to their mutual well-being, the people will finally have their priorities straight.

A real social revolution unleashes the human spirit from the shackles of oppression. When we act in agreement toward a common purpose, we are teaching, encouraging and inspiring each other rather than fighting for a position above one another. Some will take the lead, others will follow and everyone will cooperate. When people waste time with bickering and trickery, they are taking a step backward on the Road to Success. Enlightened people move forever forward and never back. Taking one step ahead is two steps ahead of taking one step back.

Consider 5,000 years of patriarchy and 250 years of modern women's suffrage and equal-rights movements. Patriarchy continues dying a long hard death. There's still a long way to go, yet rather than waiting for the rest of the world to grant equal rights and opportunity to all people, enlightened societies can be bastions of social and racial equality. We will not operate as a patriarchy or a matriarchy; rather an equalarchy.

The ultimate social revolution is achieved by banishing hatred. Hatred is the destroyer of dreams. Hatred is the great divider. The highest destination is reached by cultivating love. Love is the fulfiller of dreams. Love is the great uniter. What we hate will come back to haunt us. What we love will come back to help us in our time of need. Love dissolves, displaces, and then finally replaces hatred. When hatred is gone from the house, love becomes easier. When pursuing love, the means are the ends. Loving one another is the only practice that makes real sense. Once love becomes a way of life, we won't want it any other way. Once harmony holds sway, the people will no longer be living in the Animal Kingdom where attitudes reflect suspicion, and are necessarily defensive and protective. We will dwell in the Human Kingdom where our attitudes are joyful, open and receptive.

8.–Local Political Revolution

For most citizens, governments are unapproachable, remote institutions. They are not organizations we feel a valued part of. There are many political forces tearing societies apart, so it makes perfect sense for good people to establish their own local governments better able to banish those negative forces. You cannot easily change your Federal or State governments, but people can have a significant effect on what's going on locally. The *Declaration of Independence* is clear about the universal right to rebel against oppressive government:

> Governments are instituted among men, deriving their just powers from the consent of the governed, that when any form of government becomes destructive of these ends, it is the right of the people to alter and abolish it, and to institute new government, laying its foundations on such principles, and organizing its powers in such form, so as to them shall seem most likely to affect their safety and happiness.

The next American Revolution can begin with local governments that truly realize the American ideals of liberty and justice for all. Political pioneers can declare independence

from both the greedy businesses and the divided governments that lower our quality of life. This book outlines a
plan for a local revolution pursued in the spirit of the *Declaration of Independence*: a small-scale revolution forming
limited-scale autonomous governments of *good people*, by
good people and for *good people*.

Restless shareholders of a prospering people's corporation
that is nearing the limits of its growth will be yearning for a
fresh challenge. Adventurous members can focus their momentum on the next frontier: a people's corporation developed on a remote parcel of land: a *private-commonwealth
municipality*. Such an independent, highly autonomous
colony will gather a full set of companies and estates in one
location to establish the ultimate civilization-scale human
environment engineered to last into the far future. A private-commonwealth municipality is a private community
working with and within a county, state and federal government. It strives to combine the best of rural and urban living
by maintaining the tranquility of rural life and the lower cost
of small-town living while developing a vibrant downtown
with shopping, dining and entertainment akin to a much
bigger city.

Once a municipality is fully developed, each of its one
hundred estates sends a representative to *the General Council*
of one hundred. General Councils will be regular gatherings
of select members who represent both their estate and com-

pany interests. Each of the one hundred council members will represent the other ninety-nine members of their estate. Every voice will be heard: some directly, most indirectly. There will be no lobbyists walking the halls of power. There will be no election campaigns and no political advertising.

A private-commonwealth municipality will be able to create a significantly higher quality of life than any public government. There will be no one hoarding resources or mis-informers manipulating the masses. There will be no big-box stores, payday lenders or pawn shops. There will be no darkness at the edge of town, no slums or bums. Everyone will be an enfranchised, entitled, plugged-in, tuned-in participant—creating, producing and cultivating their talents in a dynamic local economy. Members will have access to a wide variety of common resources for their education, recreation and entertainment. It won't get too congested, except on festival days.

Coming up—a great adventure. Ahead in the distance—a glorious destination. This story ends over the hills and far away in the greatest civilization. Your Avalon, Shangri-La, Emerald City, Atlantis, Kings Landing—Call it what you like. This love story has a happy ending. Good drama calls for impassable roadblocks and insurmountable setbacks, but there are no bad guys in this tale. Rest assured there will be plenty of roadblocks and obstacles on your journey to local harmony. Meanwhile, please be my guest and grant yourself the guilty pleasure of luxuriating your curious mind in an extravagant daydream of a better life for yourself and everyone who joins you.

Two

FUTURISM

1.–Time

O nce upon a time long ago, the Universe exploded into motion. Ever since it settled down, it has remained in perpetual motion keeping time like a cosmic clock. The Earth rotates and revolves around the Sun marking precise time. At any given moment in time, people can either go backward in their memories or forward in their imaginations. People can fantasize about time travel, yet no mystical viewing screens or magical powers grant anyone the ability to glimpse even a few seconds ahead. We know time flies when we're having fun and drags when we're not. Time is used to measure every aspect of our lives. Time is a part of every rate (speed, wages, interest, inflation, etc.). Time is an essential factor in every business equation. Investors, executives, economists and bankers are rewarded for accurately anticipating what will happen in the time to come. Time is a prime factor in physics equations that elucidate the structure of the Universe.

Contemplating the future is a uniquely human activity. Youngsters are ceaselessly pestered about what they want to be when they grow up. Teens are admonished to seek a higher education and plan a career. Freshly minted college graduates inspired by the magic of compound-interest earnings and tall tales of fortunes made playing the market are urged to save for their retirement even before they've left the commencement ceremony.

We soon learn that no matter how we strive to get ahead, plenty of distractions can get in the way. After all, the future is but an idea and there is way too much fun to be had today. While many young people begin with the best of intentions; the difficulties of meeting obligations and sticking to plans can feel insurmountable. For so many, the future appears bleak, and planning seems a futile affair, but only those who plan for better days to come can harbor any realistic hope for a distinctly better future.

Is humanity condemned to repeat the past or is there something better around the next bend? It can never be the way it was. It cannot stay the way it is. So, how is it going to be? Even though one might assume the human race is becoming smarter and wiser every day, there is much evidence to the contrary. Some of us avoid thinking about the future because the present is so difficult while many others resign themselves to humankind's inevitable demise and are happy eating, drinking and making merry till they die. Fortunately, a few brave people will embrace the challenge—no matter what the odds for success.

There is no way back. We cannot flee into the wilderness to escape civilization and expect to find the happiness we seek. The way forward harkens backward to an old rule-book—before slavery, before sexism, before rulers coerced subjects, before overpopulation and urban over-expansion. World history can be studied like an encyclopedia of the human experiment from which to draw lessons for a better future. Science and technology continually progress, while the success of human societies has oscillated between magic and tragic since the beginning of civilization.

Trailblazers will be confronting the Old World by try-ing to establish a new one. They must prepare well for the journey ahead and all the hatred, narrow-mindedness and ignorance they are likely to encounter. Wise pioneers wait for clarity before making any serious moves. They are building big ships. Who will be at the helms of these ves-sels when crossing stormy waters? The captains of these ships must be thoroughly prepared to confront adversity and overcome obstacles with every gram of intelligence and ounce of passion they can summon. Conflicts and difficul-ties are lessons-to-be-learned, bridges-to-be-burned on the long road ahead.

Journalists chronicle and analyze current events. Historians investigate the past to better understand the world today. In contrast to the confusion of current events or the rich, dense drama of history, futurists claim a license to dream. Designing a better future is a fun, challenging and constructive mental exercise that fully engages the imagination and challenges one's mental capabilities. Futurism draws on a full spectrum of academic fields, such as history, anthropology, sociology, psychology, business, economics, political science, architecture and urban planning.

If one were to dismiss history's profoundest thinkers for their worst ideas, there would be few people left to venerate. Most renowned philosophers and political leaders have at one time or another espoused a strange mixture of enlightened and unenlightened ideas, as if they had one foot in the future and the other in the past. Aristotle believed the brain was a radiator of sorts that cooled the body. Thomas Jefferson championed the pursuit of life, liberty and happiness; but once he died, his slaves were sold at auction to pay off the debts he incurred for his sumptuous retirement. Napoleonic law ended feudalism throughout Europe while back home in Paris, Napoleon suppressed freedom of the press. Woodrow Wilson advanced his Fourteen Points and League of Nations yet issued executive orders racially re-segregating Washington D.C. after fifty years of integration. For trailblazers to truly be on the path to an enlightened society, they must have both feet stepping toward the future.

Futurism is not a particularly quixotic, exotic or esoteric pursuit. We all spend time planning for our own future, and everyone has contemplated the future of the world. The aim of the futurism outlined in this book is to synthesize a comprehensive local scheme for a better future for humanity. The specific goal is to be on the leading edge of history by establishing small, state-of-the-art civilizations—havens of harmony meant to inspire regional, national and international harmony. While many people's lives will remain anchored in the past, seekers of a new horizon can thrive in a society that defines the future. Romantic notions of grand civic improvement or living in an idyllic country locale aside; this book presents a solid investment scheme to create a prosperous and peaceful future. Much of the futurism presented in the pages ahead is not very futuristic. This plan is about the next step in human progress—pioneering a harmonious way to prosper.

2.–Declare Your Independence

Most news, non-fiction literature, cultural commentary and political criticism centers on famous people and big organizations. There is a truckload of literature about the relentless drama and trauma of people in power. This book is not about them. This is about us and what we can do to play our part shaping a better future. The greatest falsehood of our time is people can never really get along. Naysayers will claim local harmony can't happen. Skeptics will continue to claim it's impossible for people to work and live in harmony. Please prove them wrong. Declare your independence by pioneering an enlightened society where all people work together for their own good while working for everyone else's good.

People are not fundamentally good or bad. It is the environment we live in that brings out the best or the worst in us. The solution to the puzzle of human nature is simple in principle, but difficult in practice. Bringing out the best in people in a significant and sustainable way will require establishing a fundamentally different society and economy. The people ready to improve their lives in a fundamental way need a distinct plan of action. Unfortunately, there are no viable economic, social or political models that can be brought back from the past to give birth to harmonious societies in our modern world. Viable schemes for a better future, while considering ways of organizing used by past societies, must be significantly different from anything that has existed before. It's time to shift the focus from trying to reform the current system to concentrate on pioneering new systems of business and government.

Forget the fancy words, impossible daydreams and unrealistic rhetoric. Now is the time for us to put aside our differences and unify our efforts. Dreamers imagine a better world and picture themselves walking through it. They commence their thought-experiments with long and wide visions. Seekers summon their talents and conjure their Muses to inspire. They ponder what they can achieve for themselves and what they can accomplish for the greater good. Their goal is to establish an organization in which everyone thrives—to create a way of getting ahead in which no one gains at the expense of another's loss—a way in which the most dedicated and talented, rather than the most privileged, people rise to the top.

Consider the full range of life's possibilities from the worst to the best. Your life probably falls somewhere in the middle of the spectrum. In many ways, you are free. In other ways, you are a wage-slave working and living in a mutual-exploitation society. You are probably developing only a fraction of your inherent potential. You are probably experiencing only a fraction of the love you have the capacity to give and receive. You are probably making a fraction of the income you have the potential to earn. It is time to break free from the shackles that bind you and declare independence from the forces standing in the way of your progress.

Peace on Earth must begin somewhere. It has to start with someone. How about you? Establishing an egalitarian society is something worth fighting for, worth sacrificing everything you have for. Pioneers are well advised to listen to their critics and weigh any reasonable arguments. We should never believe we have a foolproof plan and forever strive to improve it.

It will take more than a rag-tag band of malcontents to form a true democracy. It will take wealthy people and not-so-wealthy people combining their wits. It will take well-connected people awakened to the concerns of the world cooperating with plenty of not-so-well-connected people afflicted by the problems of the world. It will take upper-, middle- and working-class people synthesizing their interests and combining their concerns. A grand movement to form a better society must inspire armchair intellectuals and coffee-shop savants to break away from their endless analyses and move into action.

Repentant insiders with longtime careers in questionable organizations get fed up and quit their jobs to become whistle blowers. They turn in their badge and decoder-ring, pledge allegiance to the truth and finally write a book exposing the dirty deeds they were privy to. Before you know it, a new scandal is revealed and a fresh set of criminal suspects are rounded up for questioning. Mug shots of the captured culprits frown from magazine and tabloid-newspaper covers. Local news media are sure to wring every ounce of drama out of a juicy scandal to keep viewers tuned in. The leaders in charge of cleaning up the mess vow a thorough housecleaning, yet after justice is done, the problem remains at large. It is only a matter of time until the next scandal arises. Politicians running for office never stop calling for reform. Despite eternal promises of better days to come and constant tinkering with the system, the promised reforms do not bring about the fundamental changes really needed.

There is no reason good citizens should be consistently victimized by criminals in high and low places. Honest hard-working people are forced to live in a corrupt and confused world degraded by their nefarious deeds. There is no reason we should be taxed by corruption. There is no justifiable reason we should have our freedom restricted because other people abuse theirs.

In large, poorly integrated organizations, the parts and levels are remote from one another, so no one has a clear view of the big picture. Trouble begins when enterprising individuals place their personal gain ahead of organizational interests. Behind closed doors, corruption grows in secret. To prevent double-dealing, this scheme focuses on the establishment of open, equal, limited-scale organizations in which everyone is fully aware of everything going on. Everyone will benefit from the free flow and open sharing of knowledge. There will be no obscure parts of the organization where corruption can take root. When we work toward a common, mutually beneficial goal, there will be few incentives to work against the common cause.

One of the reasons people are so at odds with one another

is because the world is still full of people who do not communicate well. Difficulties persist when communication is not open and free. Consider disenchanted workers who desire a fair hearing to express their concerns. They know their bosses can be very touchy and have little interest in what they have to say, so they approach the situation cautiously. They keep their thoughts to themselves hoping for a convenient moment to speak their mind. Somehow, that moment never comes. The truth is never acknowledged, and the problem is never discussed. When communication is suppressed, anger slowly brews and conflict eventually ensues. Chances are if the people are not already in the habit of freely discussing what's on their minds, it's not going to happen spontaneously. It is time for us to declare independence from those who do not communicate well to stake our claim working with supportive people who are committed to communicating well.

The simple solution to so many relationship problems is for everyone involved in the organization to hold discussions on a regular basis. Transparency is not an important part of the plan for most organizations. In egalitarian organizations, discussing every relevant issue is the centerpiece of the gameplan. After the people let go of all the nonsense that inhibited them from communicating openly, they're going to have a big laugh over all the trivial hang-ups and misunderstandings that got in the way before.

A classless society has the potential to prosper far better than a traditional stratified society that perpetually sets people against one another. The people at the top of a stratified society profit from the exploitation of people at the bottom. When we are truly united in purpose, we can harmonize everyone's economic, social, political and spiritual differences. We can satisfy both our material desires and our spiritual needs to achieve both harmony and prosperity.

It won't come easy. Halfway through, many frustrated seekers will be wondering why they ever got involved in challenging escapades to save the world. They may feel a strong urge to quit and walk away. Although I may make pioneering an egalitarian business system and establishing a true democracy sound rather simple, it will not be an easy task. Some of my readers will pause to take note of my classic use of reverse psychology—to tacitly encourage you by discouraging you. Just keep this in mind—ideas are one thing—turning those ideas into a more prosperous and harmonious way of life will prove challenging.

Great minds think great thoughts. Great minds can imagine harmony, engineer harmony and design harmony. Some people dream of climbing the highest mountain to discover the deepest seclusion for the profoundest mystical contemplation. It's time for seekers to come down from their mountain hideaways to unify their visions and focus their efforts.

A framework of local harmony is what we shall build in

the pages ahead. Your mission—should you decide to accept it—Be a pioneer. Be a starter. Be a leader. Some people relish taking the lead, most are content to follow. Curious but risk-averse people will wait on the sidelines until our enterprise system shows promise. Some people who were initially excited may lose interest while others who were most skeptical to begin with will become the most dedicated over the long run.

If you are inspired to organize, by all means, fire people up. Get your friends started. Show them the way. Leaders conceive decisive plans of action and outline clear visions that inspire others to join. Great leaders are great listeners. Imaginative leaders weave new thought-garments from many threads of inspiration. Wise leaders play puzzle master deciphering the best way to fit the pieces of the human jigsaw together.

There is no X to mark the spot on this treasure map. The buried treasure we seek will be discovered in the awakening of the hearts and minds of the heartbroken and the satisfaction of their passionate yearning for a better life. Long-term visions are a tough sell. There is no instant gratification pursuing challenging ventures to save the world. No magic wand is on offer. I promise no magic carpet ride, except in your imagination. Peace seeking pioneers think big. They think beyond their lifetimes. They think above and beyond the petty concerns, trivialities and nonsense afflicting their daily lives. They do not want this life to be just a dream that passed them by. Somebody is going to shape the future. This is your invitation to be one of those people.

3.—A Science of Ourselves

The first humans beheld in wonder the pristine natural world they inhabited. They marveled at the grace of the birds, the industry of the insects, the cunning of the big cats and the marauding mass of the mastodons. Compared to the avatars of the animal world; human strength, speed and elegance was feeble, so primitive people strove to emulate the abilities of the animals they admired. The primeval forest was alive with the music of birds and insects while the first people could do little more than grunt and moan. Inspired to join the natural soundtrack, they fashioned drums and flutes and learned to sing. Inventive craftsmanship and cunning tactics gave early humans an edge. They survived by their wits. What they lacked in strength and speed, they made up for with strategy and innovation.

The first people captured and controlled fire. Perhaps a brave soul grabbed a burning branch after a lightning strike, brought it back to camp and kept its flame alive. This gift from the Sky Gods established a place to stay for the night. Developing a portable way to start fire was a quantum leap forward for hunter gatherers. Fire was a wonder to ancient people—heat and light radiating from the crackling, ferocious, destructive and creative process of wood burning. Fire provided warmth. Fire gave light. Fire was fun to play with. Fire was the primitive TV set. If the fire went out by morning, it could quickly be brought back to life by fanning buried embers to set fresh kindling alight.

Fire gave birth to industry. The Stone Age ended when people discovered how to use fire to melt certain rocks into metals. Plains Indians burned field and forest to expand their hunting grounds. Many iconic North American large mammals: the mastodon, saber-tooth tiger, giant sloth and pygmy elephant went extinct shortly after the first humans showed up in North America more than 13,000 years ago.

By chance, experimentation and discovery, people have continually sought to improve their lives and extend their abilities—all by way of science. Over the past century and a half, humankind invented aircraft, telecommunications and submarines. However squalid or magnificent, science creates the world we live in. People long dead and beyond account invented their way into the mess of the modern world. People of this present generation must invent their way out of this mess. It's time to get creative by using science to design and build civilizations that fulfill all our needs with minimal harm to our fellow creatures and the natural environment we all live in.

Science is a Latin word for knowledge. Science is the discovery, expression and application of knowledge. People living today are the inheritors of a million years of hominid discovery and experimentation. Without science, it would be back to square one—banging rocks together. All cognizant people are scientists of a sort using knowledge to negotiate their daily struggles and chart a course for their life. As knowledge grows, each person can only comprehend a smaller fraction of a greater whole. Each branch of science has become so specialized, no particular science looks at the big picture of the human condition.

As the world turns, knowledge grows, technology progresses, yet human nature remains the same. Despite the ceaseless growth of knowledge and the boundless possibilities of technology, humankind has gravely failed to solve a long list of perennial problems—widespread ignorance, endemic poverty and endless cycles of violence to name a few. A science of ourselves would appear to be fundamental. Despite the accelerating growth of knowledge, it seems we have lost sight of ourselves and the destructive society we all are forced to participate in. We've allowed our better nature and our dreams to fall prey to the notion that a better society doesn't require us as individuals. By remotely controlling each other, people have become abstractions to one another. Behind sleek modern veneers, much of our "civilized" behavior is Stone Age. Evil minds sprout the cleverest excuses to justify their wholly self-interested actions. Obsessed with out-maneuvering their rivals, devious people descend to ever-lower levels of nefariousness. Mesmerized by their cherished delusions, zealots grow deaf to other points of view, irrevocably adamant about the misperceptions they use to justify their irrational actions.

We humans are obsessed with ourselves. Other people are the most beautiful and the ugliest creatures in the world. Picture a downtown newsstand or the home page of your favorite news site. Most of the pictures are of people: famous and infamous, heroic and criminal, celebrated and demonized. Snoop around and listen in on most any conversation. People are talking about what other people did, how it affects them and their relationships, and what they're planning to do about it. Relationships of every kind are a central concern in human affairs. Bad relationships are the beginning of so many problems; therefore, better relationships can put an end to many problems.

We should pursue a science of ourselves for the purpose of creating superior organizations in which everyone can thrive and no one is marginalized. Let pioneering people re-assemble the pieces of the human puzzle into a unified, harmonized whole. Many things have come between us that prevent us from living better lives. Let human scientists figure out exactly what those things are (and how to get them out of the way) so the people can fully resolve the disharmony between each other for all time. It's about time science is used to solve the ultimate challenge of how to generate more love.

Calling all scientists–! Let's use science to save the Planet Earth for real. What's the use of all this technology if people use that technology to destroy our beautiful planet? What's the use of all this knowledge if people cannot finally use science toward the greatest good of all?

4.–Human Evolution

Charles Darwin's scientific masterwork *On the Origin of Species*, published in 1859, spawned a perennial debate between the ancient idea of creation and the modern theory of evolution. Perhaps these concepts are not the polar opposites they are traditionally characterized to be. Were human beings created or did people evolve? Perhaps the answer is both—Humans were created and people are evolving. Humankind are an evolving creation. If this world is a creation—What or who is its creator? How we came into being is still a mystery, and I remain content to leave it as such for now. My real concern is—What are we evolving into? Toward what end is humanity progressing, as a species and a planetary society?

The shiny steel ball circumnavigating the roulette wheel of life landed in our slot. Homo sapiens are evolution's masterpiece. Human beings are blessed with the royal flush of characteristics that enable us to flourish like no other animal. Primitive peoples had a rough start. They had to summon their wits and marshal their resources or perish in the harsh wilderness. The challenges and hardships they faced inspired the search for better ways to feed, clothe and shelter themselves. Over countless generations, humankind developed the knowledge and technology to rise to the top of the food chain.

As a result of humankind's long, hard-won scientific and technological evolution, we can fulfill basic needs and get our work done with incredible efficiency. Modern technology grants us more time to enjoy leisure and pursue higher callings. Nowadays, we can do more, know more and therefore be more human than any people before us. Yet the evolution of technology is a two-edged sword. We can do everything better and faster, whether helpful or harmful. We can build it bigger and better, and now we can also blow it up bigger and better than ever before.

It is often said that people use a small fraction of their brainpower. Each person has an inherent potential that is rarely fully realized. Yet no one is ignorant or poorly skilled because they wanted or chose to be. The problem is an exploitation-driven society that wastes people's time, robs their peace of mind and endlessly distracts them with useless information and mindless entertainment. The notion of "survival of the fittest" has been hijacked by devious people, even Ivy-League-educated executives, who contrive highly twisted rationales to justify their manipulations. Yes indeed, the fittest do survive under hostile circumstances, yet predatory environments are exactly what enlightened people do their best to avoid. Let's set things straight once and for all time: "Survival of the fittest" is never a viable justification for people to use their advantages against other people. We are not *in the jungle* anymore. We are not *of the jungle* anymore. Nothing good comes from humankind preying on their own species.

People possess the power to drive one another crazy. We also have the power to drive one another sane. People have the power to thwart their evolution. People also have the power to turbo-charge their mutual evolution by tapping into the latent powers of the human heart and soul. Seekers of the truth open their hearts and minds to evolve. Surrounded by encouraging people, being open is easy. If someone has a question, we ask it. When someone else has an idea, they share it. When creative people put their minds together, they discover a reservoir of inspiration—a fountain of (you)thful ideas. Crazy ideas. Fun ideas. Impossible ideas. Strange ideas. Sharing ideas inspires better ideas. Creativity is the fruitful ambrosia of a light, lucid, playful spirit. A creative spirit elevates the mood. Inspired people take advantage of an elevated spirit to evolve to their fullest.

5.–Knowledge and Wisdom

The human race is far older than any national, religious, ethnic, or tribal identity. Humankind is a single species divided by shallow identities that perpetuate limiting self-definitions and strengthen narrow associations. After drifting so far apart for so long, it is time for humanity to come back together in a meaningful way by transcending the insignificant and outdated identities that divide us. It is time to forsake obsolete traditions that divide societies to pioneer fresh traditions that bring people together and keep them together.

Knowledge is all we know. Wisdom is the prudent use of knowledge toward the good of all. Philosophy is the elucidation of wisdom. Philosophy has ancient roots in Greece, India and China. All three rose to an early peak nearly 2,500 years ago. Pythagoras, the Buddha and Confucius were near contemporaries. Since then, philosophy has played a central role in shaping societies, civilizations and governments. The American system of government was inspired by a distinct set of Enlightenment philosophers: Locke, Montesquieu, Rousseau, Voltaire and Smith.

Popular self-help books characterize spiritual enlightenment and higher consciousness as lofty, elusive, and nearly impossible attainments. Higher consciousness, as considered here, is simply the collective consciousness achieved by openly and freely communicating about common pursuits. Spiritual enlightenment is no enigma after all. Spiritual enlightenment is achieved by reconciling our differences and practicing our highest values by mutually supporting one another's efforts.

Wise people are commonly characterized as rare characters of untold brilliance able to solve baffling problems beyond the grasp of the common person. In reality, most wisdom is common sense practiced in everyday situations. The knowledge required to establish a harmonious civilization is vast and complex and draws upon many fields of study. The practical wisdom required is rather simple. Wisdom is of little use until put to use, and the greatest wisdom is realized when people cultivate harmonious relationships by taking advantage of human nature to their mutual advantage.

Most of us are too proud to admit how sensitive we are. Behind defensive façades pushing everyone away, we are vulnerable creatures craving connection. Perhaps 3,000 years of philosophy can be summed up with the simple proposition that throwing rocks at one another does not produce the ideal outcome. It's time to stop throwing rocks and sit down to discuss how to cooperate to make the most of what we have.

Knowledge is to human beings as air is to birds. People are so busy, they seldom pause to appreciate the knowledge they use every waking moment of their life. Consider the origin, use and transmission of information. Then ask yourself why and how it is distorted. Devious people use what they know to take advantage of ignorant people—they know a sucker when they meet one. Deceitful people abuse their expertise to distort, twist and hide the truth to persuade. Devious people exaggerate to alarm and anger to influence. Misleaders distort knowledge to maintain control over their followers.

Knowledge without wisdom can be a dangerous thing. Greed-driven, egotistical motives to learn pervert the beauty of education—How ironic. Evil deeds are continually done by well-educated people—How tragic. The world is being destroyed by some of its best and brightest—How inexcusable. Eloquent words are readily employed to justify the stupidest things. In a peace-purposed education system, wisdom will be built into every relevant aspect of education. Harmony happens when people use what they know for healing and constructive purposes. Peace blossoms when education is universal and knowledge is used for the good of all.

Poor in knowledge, the people cannot prosper. The people cannot thrive when the information they need is chained in the dictator's dungeon. Knowledge needs to be free to roam to sow the seeds of eternal growth in distant homes. When it is liberated, accurately transmitted and intelligently applied, the people will live in the light of its magic to pursue fuller, more satisfying and creative lives. Restricting knowledge is like clogging arteries. Poor circulation prevents it from getting to where it is needed most. In open and curious cultures, everyone is a teacher of what they know and a student of what they yearn to learn. When all we know is freely discussed and fully used toward everyone's benefit, knowledge will grow and wisdom can flourish.

Enlightened people value wisdom above all. Wisdom is better than weapons of war. Wisdom encourages the cultivation of love—the one thing people can still agree there is just too little of. Enlightened people are wise to love and love to be wise. They form a love family. They treat their brother like a brother. They treat their sister like a sister. They treat their elders and minors with respect and courtesy.

A true union cannot have two rule books. A genuine union does not play by a double standard, rather it observes one simple Golden Standard. Equality is the key to social harmony. Equal from the beginning, an egalitarian society will not constantly struggle to balance their human equation. This is the great secret formula, hidden from the ages, and finally revealed—Openness and equality are the route to harmony—And it only gets better from there. Are you ready?

Three

Universality

1.–Universal Local Culture

About 100,000 years ago, human beings began wandering northward and eastward out of Africa into Europe and Asia. Over the next 90,000 years, people ventured to the far ends of the planet. The global trek was complete when a band of adventurers reached the southern tip of South America about 10,000 years ago. All along these migratory routes, various groups settled down while others kept on moving. Settled people developed their own languages, cultures and unique ways of understanding the world. Ensconced in their valleys, thriving on their plains, happy on their islands; for thousands of years, most people were unaware other civilizations even existed. Without writing, any memories of tribal origins lasted a few hundred years at best. Long ago and in many places, people lost the memory of their common origin.

At the crossroads of long-established trails, people traded their wares and indulged one another's curiosities. Trading networks expanded as populations grew and explorers discovered promising territories farther afield. While people were trading goods, they also exchanged ideas and stories. The cross-cultural fertilization of inventions and discoveries enriched industrious societies. Certain innovations, agricultural products and even particular words spread throughout the world and were adopted by almost every culture.

A rather long list of discoveries and inventions have become universal to human life in the civilized world today. Electricity is universal. Money is a universal medium of exchange. Dozens of currencies are exchanged across the globe around the clock. Fossil-fuel-powered internal-combustion engines drive most of the vehicles on the road and vessels in the water. Coffee, chocolate and bread are available everywhere. The seven-day week, twelve-month year, sixty-minute hour and twenty-four-hour day are universal.

Certain words coined once upon a time are universal to most languages spoken today. Although no word is found in every culture, expressions such as *okay* and *huh,* and words such as *taxi, police* and *television* are understood everywhere. Arabic numerical symbols are universal. Standardized weights and measures synchronize science and industry. Alphabets ease written communication. Everyone laughs and smiles to express happiness, claps to show approval, and sheds tears of sadness and tears of joy. The human heart is universal, for each one yearns for the same things.

Every nation, state and municipality faces challenging problems, such as conserving limited resources, reducing pollution, controlling crime, promoting employment and trade. People everywhere in the civilized world are dealing with the same issues: earning enough to make a happy home then finding the time and resources to pursue their dreams. In a billion households—speaking a thousand languages—families are dealing with parallel issues: raising the kids, paying the bills and planning for the future. Too many barriers tragically prevent us from uniting to solve our common problems.

In authoritarian cultures, the leader, the preacher or the teacher orates, preaches or teaches. When they're done, they seldom have time to answer our challenging questions. There is no feedback. Listeners are not encouraged to think for themselves. They are instructed to: *Take it or leave it—Believe it or not*. In closed-minded, close-hearted cultures, the communication is one way. In open-minded, open-hearted cultures, the communication is all ways. Universal cultures see humankind as one extended family engaged in one universal struggle for local harmony and planetary peace.

As *attached-to* or *identified-with* their culture as anyone may be, no culture is very old on the timeline of human history. Universal cultural pioneers strive to liberate themselves from outdated ideas and unhealthy attachments. Most human problems are universal—hence solutions can be universal—local, yet universal. By observing a mutually beneficial standard of conduct, our people can establish harmony within our communities. The people strive to live in a way that if everyone lived that way, peace on Earth would prevail.

The United States of America was settled by proud immigrants from every other country on Earth. Newly arrived foreigners gravitate to the enclaves pioneered by their countrymen. Many ethnic neighborhoods feature community centers and houses of worship. On the avenue, signs display messages in strange foreign scripts with English subscripts to guide visitors. Unusual aromas waft from colorful bakeries and fantastic restaurants. Exotic food stores cater to people longing for a taste of home.

People cannot intentionally synthesize fresh local cultures simply by rubbing up against each other and eating in one another's restaurants. However, we can purposefully synthesize fresh local cultures in much the same way we would cook a universal stew that draws from the best aspects of all our cultures. For a fresh, local cultural stew, love is the main ingredient. Although racism, sexism and violence pervade many cultures, our cooks must not allow any rotten ingredients into our universal stew. Our cooks let their stew retain all its pungent and potent local flavors yet coalesce into something very tasteful and satisfying to all our taste buds. . . . The stew is brewing. . . . Finally, cooks fetch their trusty tongs and carefully and gently pull the hatred out. With all the bitterness gone, their culinary creation is bursting with a vibrant bouquet of tantalizing flavors.

This is how we should harness the power of love—by forming societies of open-hearted, open-minded, high-spirited people who act in each other's mutual interest so they learn more, get more done and have more fun. Universal cultures are open-minded. Open minds communicate all ways crossing every invisible boundary. Universal cultures leave all the unnecessary cultural baggage behind by using science and open inquiry to guide the way forward. Open and honest societies can truly progress—closed minded and secretive societies will slowly die from suffocation.

On the leading edge of history, enlightened societies will pioneer universal cultures centered on the Golden Rule portending a New Golden Age. Everything that divides us will be discouraged. Everything that unites us will be encouraged. There will be no isolating class divisions, no marginalization and no exploitation. Peaceful pioneers will bring the epic human journey around full circle from its ancient beginnings to a new beginning to be one people again.

2.–The Mystery of Words

Crystal-clear definitions are essential to mastering the word game. In everyday, informal speech, we use the words we deem appropriate to convey our message with a clear meaning and the proper impact. In formal discourse, inquiring people might need to bone up on the definitions of key terms to meet the demands of precise communication. It's time well spent. A better understanding of words leads to a more nuanced use of language. Clarifying the meanings of words may be confusing at first yet is essential for accurately analyzing and solving problems.

When the way a word is used drifts too far from its formal meaning, the definitions wayward speakers discover in the dictionary may surprise them. Lexicographers, the scholars who compose definitions and compile dictionaries, are tireless chroniclers of the meanings of words. Dictionaries universalize the understanding of words. Established definitions facilitate greater accuracy in written and spoken communication. To clarify the full understanding of a word, it is essential to distinguish how one informally uses and associates that word (its connotations) from how that word is defined in the dictionary (its denotations). Listen carefully next time a passionate dispute erupts. Often the argument is not over the issue itself, the real debate is over the definition of a keyword.

Perhaps we can bring some clarity to four hot-button words: *liberal*(ism), *conservative*(ism), *socialism* and *capitalism*. The way these terms are bandied about in popular discourse can be cringeworthy. A deeper dive into these words should liberate them from any negative connotations and conserve an accurate sense of their meanings.

Liberal

The adjective *liberal* means generous; tending to give freely. Politically, *liberal* connotes being open to new ideas and favoring reforms guided by social science and the quest to uphold the common decency of all people. The word *liberal* is closely related to the words *liberate* which means to set free from oppression, confinement or control, and *liberty*: freedom from oppression. In Europe, liberalism was born out of people striving to liberate themselves from the oppression of monarchy, aristocracy and Church. Liberalism as a political theory promotes the freedom of individuals to pursue their passions, express themselves and live the lives they choose. Classical liberalism espouses free speech, free assembly and free markets with limits set by laws to ensure the wellbeing of the people. Liberal social movements have been driven by noble motives to create fairer and more just societies by resolving their inequalities and injustices.

The classification of the United States as a liberal democracy is made clear in the preamble to the Constitution, which expresses liberty as its supreme value:

> We the People of the United States, in order to form a more perfect union, establish justice, ensure domestic tranquility, provide for the common defense, promote the general welfare, and secure the Blessings of Liberty to ourselves and our Posterity, do ordain and establish this Constitution of the United States of America.

The greatest liberation in American history was the emancipation of the slaves during the Civil War. The Progressive Era of the early twentieth century spawned the next great series of liberations. Child labor was outlawed, clean food standards were established, labor unions gained power and women secured the right to vote—all features of society we take for granted today.

Franklin Roosevelt's New Deal Legislation, which provided relief for citizens suffering during the Great Depression and introduced fundamental reforms, was another high point in the progress of liberalism. Labor unions were empowered, social security was established, and government played an active role putting people to work on grand public projects. The post-war economic revival based on liberal policies brought about the longest sustained period of economic growth in American history. The last high point of liberalism was the Civil Rights Movement of the 1960s which inspired the Civil Rights Bill of 1964 and the Voting Rights Act of 1965.

Political liberals are not (never) happy with the status quo and believe more change is called for. They continue to focus on the plight of the working class and the struggles of not-so-fortunate members of society. Liberals are weary of the abuses of big business and the exploitation of the environment. They are generally more supportive of marginalized groups who challenge social norms. For liberals, the freedom for people to discover who they are and explore who they want to be is the very essence of the American way of life.

Liberal is a dirty word in some circles, yet I suspect most people who hold a strong disdain for political liberalism are ignorant of its definition and unaware of its history. Most generalizations of liberal political policies are misleading. Efforts to help the poor, promote fairness and fight for justice are for the most part constructive. Blaming the poor for their poverty is misguided. Just as nobody made a personal choice to be overweight, ignorant or disabled; no one is poor because they wanted or chose to be. Demonizing the lowest members of society does not inspire innovative solutions for improving the lives of struggling people.

The liberalism that burst onto the scene and dominated

the 1960s and 70s tended toward extremes with out-of-control drug use and unhinged sexual liberation. The liberalism born in the 1960s also spawned a lot of positive changes: the anti-war movement, the Civil Rights Movement, the Environmental Movement and the better-health movement. Today's liberals hold the line supporting worker's rights, universal healthcare, diplomacy over war, solid public education, and strong environmental oversight.

American liberals can be an odd bunch. Quite a few liberals fail to see that being altruistic does not necessarily make them good people. There is no shortage of liberal snobs who rarely practice the values they proclaim. Liberals are generally not very religious; and if they are, they are drawn toward exotic spiritual practices or non-mainstream Christian denominations. Liberals tend to be dismissive of traditions and fearful of institutions. For most liberals, patriotism is an outdated concept, yet liberals love their country despite their complaints. They tend to become consumed by distress over the inequities of society.

To the restless and discontent, liberalism can be attractive. Fighting the system is rebellious. Seeking liberation is romantic. Liberalism in America is often perceived to be hipper, cooler, trendier, bendier—like tattoos, piercings or punk rock. In a world with so much wrong, being a radical nonconformist just seems right. For most liberals, conservatism is static, dull, sticking to the same routine, holding up the status quo, yearning for a past that has passed. A treatise espousing a radically novel form of government and society is by its nature rather liberal. Yet this plan aims *to conserve* all that is good and return to a time that resembles a bygone world many long for, when people were more considerate, honest and hardworking.

Conservative

To conserve means to protect from harm; to preserve. People overwhelmed by a changing world naturally long to preserve what they hold dear. People who have grown used to having things a certain way are prone to want to keep it that way. Classical conservatism recognizes how most established traditions, theories and methodologies were developed over extensive periods of time through an arduous process of trial and error. When considering changing any long-established way of doing things, one is well advised to be careful when altering something that has worked well for a long time. Things were done a certain way for particular reasons, and it is wise to learn those reasons before making changes.

Cultural conservatives live more traditional lifestyles. The children of conservatives are likely to follow in their parent's footsteps and settle close to home. Conservatives tend to be religious and dress conventionally. They are proud to be Americans and consider themselves patriots. For conservatives, preserving the traditions and values people have worked so hard to establish is the whole point of the American dream and the American way of life. Identifying as conservative feels sensible, safe, stable—following a well-trodden pathway. Political conservatives take pride in being realistic. They espouse a noble set of values centered on self-determination and hard work. They generally favor capital over labor and support a hands-off approach to business.

Conservatives are proud of the American military, which is often in direct opposition to liberals who see war as an outdated practice. Most conservatives are sane, sober, well-mannered, well-meaning people. They mistrust the rabble rousers and big-city protesters. Conservatives are more likely to own guns. They see hunting as their God-given right. Conservatives tend to keep it simple while liberals can't help but make things complicated because they are drawn to a more nuanced approach.

People who grew up in happy conservative households tend to uphold their conservative values. People who grew up in unhappy conservative households are more likely to perceive their parent's conservatism as flawed and adopt more liberal values. People who were raised in isolated conservative societies tend to become more liberal once they get out in the world. Many college students adopt more liberal values as their education broadens their perspective.

A bird cannot fly if it does not have both a right wing and a left wing working in coordination. Open forums bringing liberal and conservative viewpoints together can stimulate lively and constructive debates. Once the partisan bickering is toned down, the smoke clears, the name calling ends, and the conspiracy nuts are shown the door, reconciling liberal and conservative political values and concerns can inspire novel solutions and intelligent compromises. An enlightened society's goal is for the truth to prevail and for love to win the day. When the priority of a debate is clarifying the facts, identifying the problems and crafting the best solutions, it hardly matters what the liberal or conservative talking points were at the start.

Socialism

Socialism means collective ownership. Socialism as a political movement strives for an equitable society in which workers get their fair share. Socialist movements are driven by the simple principle that the solution to inequality is to promote equality. It makes no sense for a few people to have too much while a vast majority of people have too little to live a decent life. Socialism promotes more public ownership and government involvement in society to reconcile its injustices and balance its inequalities.

Christopher Columbus's well-publicized discovery of the New World inspired many discontent Europeans to plan their escape. North and South America were primeval lands ripe for order and civilization. Those unspoiled lands soon featured fast developing cities with scant opportunities for newcomers with few connections. Americans trapped on the East Coast dreamed of heading west to get a new start. In 1825, Robert Owens, a successful Scottish industrialist moved to the United States to establish a utopian community in rural Indiana. It was there that the term *socialism* was coined by the founders of the community they named New Harmony.

Modern socialism came of age with the Romantic Movement's awakening of individualism, elevation of intuition, veneration for nature and yearning to transcend limitations. Socialist ideas gained prominence as the Industrial Revolution fostered large-scale factory production, urbanization and mass transportation. *Socialism* came to be used as a blanket term for virtually all grassroots, reform-minded social movements. For more than 200 years, socialism and its variants have been the dominant philosophies driving economic, social and political change throughout the world. Historians on occasion retroactively use the term socialism to refer to social practices as far back as ancient Rome when the government fed the masses and provided free entertainment with chariot races and gladiator fights.

Leninism and Maoism retained the socialist label while deviating entirely from its grassroots spirit. Many major socialist revolutions established governments notorious for rapidly devolving into the worst totalitarian regimes: the

Soviet Union, Red China, Cuba, Nicaragua, Cambodia and Venezuela. Time and again, revolutionary leaders claimed dictatorial powers under the guise of a socialist revolution that would establish a more just and equitable society. They pledged to let go of the power they were granted once a new socialist order was established. Most socialist dictators failed to relinquish their powers.

There are many collectively owned, not-for-profit and public organizations that could readily be classified as socialist such as the Post Office or the Public Library. There's a whole lot of socialism going on at every level of government and every part of society. Military veterans enjoy socialized medical care by the Veterans Administration. People pay into the government-run retirement savings plan of Social Security. Poor and retired people receive healthcare through Medicaid and Medicare.

Some people proudly self-identify as socialists. Others believe socialism is a drain on society. Some right wingers label anyone on the left they don't like as socialist. For its extreme detractors, socialism is a disease. For others, socialism is the cure. Rarely do political identities or ideological labels give an accurate understanding of what people really believe, nor does it inspire creative solutions. Socialism is rarely the root cause of any problem because there is nothing inherently wrong with collective ownership, nor is socialism a universal solution.

Capitalism

Capitalism is using money to make more money. Capitalist enterprises are funded by investors who hope to earn a prof-it. The most prominent capitalist enterprises are engaged in mass production. Capitalist-driven industrialization has brought about a mixture of prosperity and poverty to much of the world. High-wage jobs and low-priced goods have liberated masses of people from poverty. Low-wage jobs and high-priced goods have trapped multitudes in poverty. Rampant industrialization has harmed human health and compromised the natural environment. The profit motive has inspired a lot of creativity and innovation but has also motivated plenty of exploitation and fraud.

I define the term *capitalism* literally as meaning *the use of capital*. You buy something for five dollars in the morning and sell it for ten dollars later on that day, you made five bucks. The motive to make more, to turn a little into a lot, is what drives *free enterprise* and *the free market*. Successful free-market economies are a marvel for consumers. Modern supermarkets have a broad range of food for sale to sati-ate shoppers' appetites and satisfy their culinary longings. Looking for a new outfit? A series of stores in the downtown shopping district of most towns have plenty of attractive clothing ready for you to try on.

In a D.I.Y mood? Local building suppliers and hobby

stores have the tools and materials artisans need to do their thing. Free-market competition is a powerful driver of innovation and inspiration for creativity. Ambitious entrepreneurs and aspiring inventors are relentlessly scheming and dreaming of novel ways to make better stuff. Musicians are forever composing new songs hoping for a break-out hit. Few people have qualms with free enterprise. What most dissatisfied consumers have a problem with are the monopolistic businesses that lie, cheat and steal to squash their competition and overcharge the public. What concerned citizens have a problem with are the greedy businesses that disregard the health of the environment and have little concern for the well-being of their employees.

Let's not fail to recognize that free enterprise is not the best method for providing certain essential services. Most markets, like most animals, can operate freely without harming anyone. On the other hand; some markets, like certain wild, predatory animals, need to be caged and controlled. A central concern in designing the ideal local economy is deciding which tasks are best accomplished by for-profit companies and which enterprises are best left to not-for-profit companies.

Capitalism is not the problem: exploitation, fraud and greed are the problem. The tragedy is that free enterprise's greatest beneficiaries do their best to avoid sharing their wealth and rarely show any concern for the common good.

The problem with capitalism is not making a profit, it is cheating in every way possible to maximize profits. Capitalists are not the problem. The problem is greedy capitalists who strive to deregulate, privatize and monopolize their industries regardless of the greater good.

3.–A Brief History of Utopians

Great thinkers have been observing the shortcomings of their societies and dreaming about establishing better ones since the beginning of civilization. Every caring soul who has made the world a better place in some small way may have contributed to the grand utopian project of the ages. Here we pay particular attention to four major players: Plato, Jesus, Adam Smith and Karl Marx.

The writings of Plato and Marx are broad and complex and evolved over their lifetimes. Jesus did not write or publish. What we have to go by is a succinct summation of his teachings collected by his followers. Adam Smith published two major works in his lifetime. I prefer to characterize these four thinkers as profound observers and great synthesizers rather than great originators or inventors. They all demonstrated concern for common people, touched on the psychology of human fulfillment and contributed to the search for solutions to humankind's universal problems.

The ideas of yesterday's great thinkers can be both surprisingly contemporary and shockingly outdated. Idealistic visions and grand moral codes tend to be extreme and impractical. Grand plans often contain some not-so-great ideas. Let's acknowledge profound thinkers, collect their outstanding ideas and discard their outdated ideas. We should encourage seekers to continue investigating the past to discover ideas relevant to the present and applicable toward the future. The historical figures I have chosen are not traditionally characterized as utopians because that title is principally given to writers of fictional utopias.

When historians draw conclusions, they naturally form opinions. Wise seekers are acutely aware how their opinions change over time as their knowledge grows, their experience broadens and their perceptivity deepens. While passionate learners relish the joy of knowing, they also recognize the limits of their knowledge, and lament that much of history will never be known. All significant thinkers, no matter how idealistic and well-intentioned, have had their ideas twisted around and used to justify the exact opposite of what they intended. Here we seek to understand four prominent thinkers and separate their gold from the dross.

Plato

Ancient Greece is renowned as the birthplace of democracy and is also the birthplace of political science. One of the great paradoxes of history is how the most famous lineage of classic Greek philosophers: Socrates, Plato and Aristotle did not hold democracy in high esteem. They relished criticizing the disorderly democratic government of their hometown Athens, while they reserved a great deal of admiration for the orderly military oligarchy that governed nearby Sparta.

Plato, who lived from 427 to 348 BC, was a student of Socrates and teacher of Aristotle. He fled Athens after his mentor Socrates was put to death. He spent twelve years traveling around the Mediterranean Sea to Egypt, Italy and other locales investigating a variety of governments. He wrote several books about politics, yet his masterpiece *The Republic* remains the most influential ancient treatise of political science. His protégé collected his observations in a comparative compendium called *Aristotle's Politics.*

Plato believed only the wisest and best educated should be entrusted to rule. Drawing from his experience he came to believe that government 'by the people,' was unstable because common citizens could be enthralled by demagogues and manipulated by despots. He concluded that the simple majority vote of a poorly informed populace is not the best way to make the wisest decisions. His ideal government became rule by a philosopher king.

In Plato's model republic, each citizen's placement in one of three social classes is determined by their success in a rigorous educational process. A small group of elite elders: *the Guardians* [gold class] are appointed to rule. A larger middle class of soldiers: *the Auxiliaries* [silver class] are trained to provide security. The largest and lowest class: *the Artisans* [bronze class] do all the labor. Plato believed this division into classes based on the discovery of people's abilities through education and testing would create harmony. Plato expressed his philosophy in carefully crafted works of literature. Plato's model republic is rather farfetched and impractical. Elders remain celibate, families are raised communally, and everyone is made to believe a fairy tale that each citizen is predestined for their station in life. *The Republic* is written as a dialog, and it covers a broad range of topics that include the famous *Allegory of the Cave* associating ignorance with the darkness and isolation of a cave.

The Platonic model inspired The Holy See, the governing body of the Catholic Church: the world's oldest continuously functioning international institution. The Catholic Church has been governed for 1,700 years by a Pope and a select group of Cardinals appointed for life. The United States Federal Reserve Board is similarly composed of a group of elite elders: a national chairman and twelve regional chairmen craft their policies independent of political pressure. The United States Supreme Court is similarly inspired by the Platonic Republican model.

The Ancient Greeks established the field of political science by defining the various types of governments in the ancient world, which are eerily similar to the governments of today. They described how various forms of government arose and were sustained, transformed or collapsed. Socrates and Plato lived through the twilight of two centuries of Greek democracy. Had they lived a century earlier, they likely would have had a more positive opinion of democracy.

Rome conquered Greece around 146 B.C. The Romans picked up where the Greeks left off by more carefully chronicling and more thoughtfully analyzing their politics. The Romans bequeathed humankind with a very colorful and instructive political history and commentary. Over nearly a thousand years, Rome cycled between dictatorship and republic and was led by a series of both enlightened and despotic emperors bequeathing ancient history with a colorful cast of ancient characters: Nero, Julius Caesar, Caligula, Hadrian, Trajan, Marcus Aurelius, Constantine. The causes of the collapse of the Roman Empire around A.D. 476 are still debated by historians and political scientists. The Byzantine Empire picked up where the Western Roman Empire left off and held sway for nearly another thousand years until it was conquered by the Ottomans in 1453.

Jesus

Jesus of Nazareth lived during the first three decades of the Common Era. His story and teachings were recorded by his followers, and four versions were compiled in *The New Testament* of the Christian Bible. The biographies of Jesus recounted in the Gospels leave off when he was a curious twelve-year-old boy questioning priests in the Temple in Jerusalem and pick up when he begins his ministry at about age thirty.

Jesus grew up near a significant crossroads of commerce, culture, religion and politics. His hometown, Nazareth—was four miles from Sephora: the Roman capitol of Galilee—forty miles from the bustling seaport of Caesarea—ninety miles from Jerusalem: the cultural center of Judaism—two hundred miles from Antioch: the lively cosmopolitan capitol of Syria. The Roman Empire famously featured the best road network of the ancient world while the Mediterranean Sea facilitated travel over water between many destinations on its shores and islands.

Jesus certainly spent some of his eighteen unaccounted-for years exploring the area surrounding his home. Some have surmised he embarked on a series of far-flung journeys to exotic lands, yet I suspect he had family and religious obligations that kept him pretty close to home. The young Jesus really wouldn't have to travel very far to encounter a broad spectrum of politics, culture and spiritual traditions. As a young man, Jesus was fascinated by the religions practiced, the political revolutionaries conspiring, and the philosophies being promoted. At the same time, he was disturbed by the exploitation, over-taxation and social unrest he observed.

Evidence suggests Jesus may have been inspired by spiritual traditions outside of his Jewish heritage. A version of the story of the prodigal son appears in Buddhist texts written five hundred years before the life of Jesus, one of several parallels which suggest he was influenced by Buddhism. Jesus' quirky method of teaching and his semi-voluntary martyrdom closely resembles Socrates who lived four hundred years earlier. Jesus synthesized a variety of ideas and perspectives into a simple introductory message he could recite in about twenty minutes. He experimented with different approaches to his ministry until he honed his ideas and perfected their delivery.

Most critics of Christianity conflate the Bible with the Church. The Gospels and Epistles were complete by the end of the first century, while the Western Church that canonized the books of the Bible coalesced several hundred years later. People who hold the Church in low esteem usually regard the Bible with equal disdain. Many critics of modern Christianity assume biased translations of the Bible are the source of the problem, yet the real source of the misdirection of contemporary churches is their inability to synthesize ancient wisdom with modern science and contemporary scholarship.

I consider Jesus as a utopian, and the core of his teachings as a utopian code of conduct. Jesus' message alludes to heavenly rewards: "Blessed are those who are persecuted for righteousness' sake, for theirs is the Kingdom of Heaven," yet also promises Earthly rewards: "The meek shall inherit the Earth." In any case, good behavior is a prerequisite for the ultimate reward: "I tell you, unless your righteousness exceeds that of the Scribes and Pharisees, you will never enter the Kingdom of Heaven." Jesus was emphatic about striving toward high ideals: "Be perfect as your Father in Heaven is perfect."

Jesus urged his followers to observe the highest possible standards for human conduct. Conscientious people do their best to take the high road by abiding by their highest ideals but are forced to compromise again and again to deal with the exigencies of the real world. Yet aspiring to a high moral code makes more sense than settling for a compromised one. When everyone in a community aspires to a high ethical code and benefits from its practice, it becomes possible to abide by that code. When high-minded, big-spirited behavior brings out the best in everyone, those people will enjoy the magic of loving kindness and experience happier and healthier lives.

Adam Smith

Adam Smith of Scotland who lived from 1723 to 1790 was a moral philosopher and free-market advocate best known today as the Father of Economics. He published his first major work in 1759: *The Theory of Moral Sentiments*. He argued that people have a natural capacity for moral judgment and described how they are motivated to cultivate civilized behavior to enjoy the many benefits of getting along with others. He was concerned with both the freedom of markets and the well-being of the poor. His first book earned him a prominent role in the Scottish Enlightenment.

After his first book earned acclaim, he landed a great job as tutor to a future duke, with whom he took three rather extensive tours of France. When he visited Paris, he was welcomed by prominent philosophers and authors. There he met Voltaire, Benjamin Franklin and many other notables. His far-ranging discussions in famous coffee shops and salons with prominent influencers of the Enlightenment, more than twenty years before the French Revolution, inspired the intellectual journey that led to his second masterpiece.

In 1776, seventeen years after his first book, Adam Smith published *An Inquiry into the Nature and Causes of The Wealth of Nations*. He demystified markets, employment and trade and laid out a formula for optimizing economic growth. He began by introducing a dynamic theory of wealth to countervail the prevailing concept that had held sway for many centuries. *Mercantilism* defines wealth as the amount of precious metals one was able to accumulate. Smith updated the understanding of wealth by describing how a country's wealth is based on its productive capacity.

Smith is famous for his observations and the simple conclusions he drew from them: money facilitates trade, the division of labor increases productivity, shortages cause prices to rise while surpluses cause prices to fall. He stated that economic progress is fostered by peace, fair taxes and an equitable administration of justice. He described how through trade, self-interest can benefit the common interest. He also concluded that larger populations facilitate greater specialization, efficient transportation promotes prosperity, and happy employees are more productive.

Misguided economic policy played a big role in a number of major world events such as the tax revolts that spurred the American Revolution, the credit bubble that burst into the Great Depression, the oppressive economic policies that led to World War Two, the failure of a command economy that led to the fall of the Soviet Union, and the rise of crony capitalism that enabled an autocratic Russia. Wise economic policy spurred America and Europe's post-war economic prosperity. Global trade policies and national economic policies not only have had a profound effect on national and international prosperity, they also influence political outcomes, social norms and human relations. The science of economics is commonly misunderstood and often disregarded, yet wise economic policies are essential to keeping the world running smoothly.

Karl Marx

Karl Marx was a journalist, historian, philosopher, economist and advocate for the working class who lived from 1818 to 1883. He is one of the most influential and controversial scholars of all time forever remembered by his iconic black and white, bearded image. Marx remains a lightning rod whose name is still bandied about mainly as an arch agent of evil. Marx is a complicated character—It's ashamed he's so misunderstood and misrepresented. The best we can do is separate his gold from the dross and move on with it.

There was a distinct line of socialist thinkers before Marx: Fourier, Saint-Simon, Owen, Proudhon, Blanc and Blanqui. Marx is by no means the father of socialism, rather he is the best-known socialist thinker. He recognized the power of capitalism but was dismayed by the prosperous factory owners who gained their wealth at the expense of poorly paid factory workers. Marx framed the debate over the root causes of social strife by characterizing it as a class struggle between the Proletariat and the Bourgeoisie.

To get the most out of Marx, one should begin by separating his critical analysis of capitalism from his advocacy of a particular brand of socialism and his prediction of a communist revolution. He characterized capitalism as inherently unfair and unstable and predicted its demise. In the economic system he prescribed to replace it, the state owns all the means of production and private property is done away with. Marxism and communism are associated with central planning and strict government oversight.

Marx believed workers would organize themselves and rise up in great rebellions, which did not happen the way he envisioned. Governments responsive to the plight of factory workers enacted laws to improve working conditions. Labor unions, which Marx had not anticipated, empowered workers to bargain for better wages, benefits and working conditions.

By the turn of the new millennium, Marx had been vanquished from popular discourse by the apparent triumph of capitalism. His ideas were subsequently validated by the economic downturn of 2008 when perplexed investigators (re)turned to Marx for an explanation of the Great Recession. Lo and behold; just as he described it would happen: the economic downturn demonstrated capitalism's instability and the slowdown's causes could be traced to the insatiable lust for wealth of a privileged elite. It's almost as if greedy investment bankers conspired to vindicate Marx's characterization of capitalists.

Marx's key observation described free markets as inherently unfair because over the course of time the winners grow wealthier while the losers grow poorer. In due time, he stated, the winners live in opulence while the workers become trapped in poverty. Even today in some parts of the world one can find skilled-and-experienced factory workers living in poverty.

One cornerstone concept of Marxism is the characterization of profit as theft: an astute but somewhat exaggerated characterization. The profit earned squeezing orange juice or mowing a neighbor's lawn is certainly not theft, yet profit earned by deceitful means can clearly be characterized as theft. When people are forced to pay too much for something, or are sold shoddy goods, they commonly refer to it as being *ripped off* implying profit by deceit is theft. When a medical-insurance company earns billions of dollars in profits while denying needed medical care; that money ended up in investors' bank accounts rather than being spent on healthcare.

Four

Human Science

1.–The Social Sciences

There are two types of science: soft and hard. The hard, or natural, sciences are the ones that first come to mind for most people (e.g. chemistry, biology, physics, geology, astronomy, etc.). They deal with objective phenomena that can be precisely observed and measured like stars in the sky, substances on a scale or chemicals in a test tube. The hard sciences are famous for mathematical formulas that describe precise relationships between measurable quantities such as Einstein's mass-energy equivalence equation: $E = mc^2$. The hard sciences are also known for comprehensive theories such as Charles Darwin's theory of evolution, which offer systematic explanations for mysterious natural phenomena.

The soft sciences are the social sciences, which deal with

the subjective world of human relations: psychology, economics, education, political science, anthropology and sociology. The soft sciences deal with phenomena that cannot be readily measured with scales, thermometers or stopwatches. Social scientists conduct their work using powers of observation. Eyes, ears and brains are their primary scientific instruments. Their scientific method involves doing surveys, conducting interviews and cross-referencing statistics to propose explanations and offer solutions. Social-science studies are scrutinized for the scope of their surveys, the methods employed to derive their conclusions and the possible biases of the researchers.

Social-science researchers strive to explain the enigmas of human behavior to improve social health. Important studies seek answers to issues of grave concern such as suicide, crime and mental illness. Management analysts study business practices to gauge the success of corporate policies. Behavioral economists study how policies and practices impact producers and consumers. Social-science statistics often find their way into popular discourse such as the divorce rate or this year's murder capital. Intriguing social-science characterizations like Elizabeth Kübler Ross's five stages of grief (denial, anger, bargaining, depression, and acceptance) have become common in popular culture.

Most scientific findings are not controversial because they don't strike close to home. When astronomers discover a new exploding star system, it doesn't cause a public uproar. When the conclusions of social-science studies challenge long-held beliefs or complicate easy answers, they provoke controversy. For instance, when a newly published study concludes that having guns in the home doesn't promote family safety, there is certain to be pushback from gun advocates.

Casual observers are prone to jump to conclusions such as cult members prefer to be indoctrinated, or disturbed people prefer to stay in abusive relationships or homeless people chose to be homeless. Social scientists go deeper than superficial observations and simple deductions. Social scientists do their best to decipher how people become stuck in the traps they find themselves in, and they monitor the success of solutions being experimented with to get them out of those traps.

Wise policy makers refer to social science studies to better understand problems and craft policies to address those problems. All too often, social scientists prescribe remedies that infringe on business interests when they reveal regressive labor policies, harmful environmental practices or deceptive public relations. Many businesses choose to fight against reform instead of changing their practices in light of scientific studies. Instead of conceding a loss to their bottom line, they engage lobbyists and hire public-relations firms to promote disinformation campaigns to confuse, scare and misinform the public and sway government policies. The discrediting of painstakingly conducted studies is a double loss because the work of social scientists goes to waste while the dire social problems they were striving to improve remain unresolved.

2.—A Psychology of Harmony

Of all the social sciences, *psychology*: the study of mind and behavior, is the one that most consistently captures the popular imagination. Of all the mysteries of the universe, perhaps the human mind is the greatest of them all. When hopeful approaches for *saving the planet* are advanced, it is the physical sciences of climatology and ecology most often cited. In contrast, the great challenge of *achieving peace on Earth* begins by solving the people puzzle.

Human consciousness is felt at the center of the physical sense organs, between the ears and behind the eyes, nose and mouth. Emotions are felt in the chest—in our hearts. Human consciousness is an oscillation between thinking and feeling. People think about how they feel and feel in response to what they are thinking. Much of what people express is a translation of feelings into words. When something feels wrong, we hesitate. When it feels right, we move ahead.

Human beings develop an extensive set of emotional mindsets to cope with both ordinary and extraordinary circumstances. When we are forced into an unexpected situation, we need to summon the appropriate emotional frame of mind. For example, if someone is counseling a friend possessed by volcanic anger, they must be able to summon their tranquility to talk their friend down from the proverbial ledge. When deciding how to deal with someone who has betrayed them and is pleading for forgiveness, normally kindhearted people may decide to conjure their cruel side and show no mercy.

People look to psychology to better understand their personal struggles and decipher sources of disturbing behavior. Psychological explanations may shed a little light on confusing situations yet fail to solve the matter at hand. Pithy insights such as "bullies are really cowards" are cold comfort when confronting a bully. Psychoanalysis can only go so far. After insightful explanations are elucidated, they should inspire a plan of action or a change in strategy.

A psychology of harmony needs to explore the psychology of disharmony to decipher the reasons people continue to cause one another so much pain and suffering. People have little trouble getting along in situations with no social status to contend over or spoils to be shared such as our nuclear family or a coterie of contemporaries. However, when social rank is at stake or money and power interests clash, adversarialism is almost certain to arise. When there is a lack of trust or a shortage of goodwill, animosity is likely to fester.

Is anybody carrying a copy of the *Map of the Road to Ruin*? Sure? Check your back pocket. The way things have been going lately would lead one to believe those malicious maps are in wide circulation. One of the great mysteries of human behavior is how so many people who start out with the best of intentions end up going down the wrong road. Make a list of those deceptive, seductive, enticing *on–ramps*. Where on the high road to better ways and happier days do well-meaning people go astray? What makes the Dark Side so seductive? Why are people are so easily spoiled? How does temptation win? How does power become an aphrodisiac and violence a way of doing business? Most important of all—make it as easy as you can for people who have gone astray to find the *off–ramps* so they can make a major turn-around.

The primary purpose behind a psychology of harmony is refining a set of methods for us to passionately debate our points of view and wisely manage our affairs without generating animosity. We already channel our aggressive, competitive urges in all sorts of games and sports. When we can tame our passions in the interest of coherently managing our affairs, we are well on our way to harmony.

Another critical issue we need to address is criminality. How shall we define *criminal behavior*? Each and every one of us has lied, most of us have engaged in some criminal behavior and many of us enjoy rooting for the bad guys in mob movies, but that does not make us criminals. For our purposes, criminals are people who consciously and continuously engage in malicious behavior. While most people contribute to society, criminals steal from society. While most people do their best to help, criminals have no qualms with harming others to have their way.

In an enlightened society, there will be few incentives or opportunities for criminal behavior. Most criminals will not feel comfortable surrounded by alert, aware, inquisitive people. Within a gated community, criminals will be acutely aware there is no easy escape. Doing their best to fit in with an enlightened society, they will have a hard time finding fellow criminals to scheme and dream with. Maybe they'll actually be inspired to give up their evil ways when an explosive public confession brings their inner darkness to light.

An enlightened society should never let down its guard and do everything in its power to prevent crime. When an offender is caught and in custody, the community should treat them with enough dignity to gain their trust. We should do our best to understand why offenders felt they could get away with nefarious deeds that would have harmed people who never did them any harm.

Final big question: After putting in years of hard work and accomplishing great things: What do ambitious people want in the end? What's it really all about? The simple answer is—*glory*. Ambitious people yearn to achieve something magnificent and awe-inspiring. Trouble is—once people achieve glory—they're going to want even greater glory.

3.—Economics

Your date cancelled and you're not feeling all that great tonight. You have two tickets for a hot show that mean little to you as curtain time approaches. After finding shelter underneath the marquee; as you take the tickets from your wallet, you immediately realize it's a seller's market. Others apparently recognize your suddenly single status and ask if you'd like to sell one of your tickets. Why not sell both? You ask $100 for the pair and right away someone bids $120; and out of thin air an auction begins. The people surrounding you start flashing their cash and for a moment you're confused. An eager theatergoer bids $140. What to do? A passionate thespian lets you know she's willing to pay $160. Are you going to peer into each of your bidders' eyes to divine the most deserving person in the crowd? A newcomer bids $180. Anyone outbid is walking away. Finally, off to the side, a quiet voice whispers $200. The auction ends, the highest bidder graciously hands over two crisp C-notes. Your clients are on their way to enjoy the show and you're on your way to savor your unexpected windfall.

Like it or not, market forces of supply and demand determine the prices of most of what is bought and sold. Local prosperity is determined by the ability to organize human and material resources to efficiently produce goods and services people are willing and able to purchase. Free markets are the arbiter of the prices of those goods and services as nothing is worth more than what people are willing to pay for it at the time. Hard-working people want to earn as much as possible for their work and pay fair prices for what they purchase.

Picture a traditional factory town. There are a few big, dirty factories in the valley. The workers live close by in meager conditions while the fat-cat factory owners live in opulent mansions on the hill. Now imagine an alternative vision of a valley filled with a series of small, clean workshops and factories organized in a marketplace and an industrial park owned by the people who work in them. The workers live in handsome apartment-building estates in town and spacious suburban estates on the outskirts of town.

Private commonwealths harness the power of free enterprise for the production of consumer goods, industrial goods and entertainment. They in turn control their market for healthcare, education, insurance, banking, real estate and housing. By controlling market sectors where costs tend to get out of hand, you prevent them from inflating the cost of living. So, if you want to strike it big in a people's corporation, you can open a restaurant, start a software company or establish a fashion outlet. Just beware there will be no fortune to be made in healthcare, insurance, banking or real estate. Education falls in the middle as there will be both not-for-profit and for-profit companies in the education field.

Money is not the measure of all things of value, but it comes pretty close. Pragmatists like to characterize "the economic argument," as the definitive factor in winning any debate concerning the use of resources. The economic argument for an enlightened society is simple. Using resources against one another is harmful and wasteful. Lying, cheating and stealing is bad for the economy. Honesty, fair dealing and respect for property rights are good for the local economy because everyone goes about their business with peace of mind. When goodness goes around, it comes around and pays dividends in increased creativity and productivity. When we share the economic pie, the pie grows. When a few greedy people hog the economic pie for more than their fair share, the pie shrinks. Pursuing peace and prosperity by sharing both fortunes and misfortunes yields the greatest good for the greatest number of people, so goodness wins and harmony prevails.

4.–Education

No education—no civilization. No doctors to heal you, no lawyers to get you out of a jam, no mechanics to fix your car and no stylists to cut your hair. The only things human beings know how to do at birth are breathe, cry and suck. Parents are the first teachers helping their children to walk and talk. Outside of the home, education continues at school. In the classroom, children sit at a desk peering at a blackboard learning how to count and reciting the alphabet. Education continues through engaging with family, exploring the world and playing with other kids. Without elementary education, children wouldn't be able to do anything but the simplest tasks. They wouldn't even have the vocabulary to join with their playmates who attend school.

Parents and educators should do their best to take advantage of their children's natural curiosity. If inquisitive youngsters pose questions and get satisfying answers, they will be encouraged to ask more questions. Take the kids to the zoo, and they'll have a hundred questions. Take them to the aquarium and they'll have a hundred more.

Most youngsters are itching to participate in what adults are doing. Often, they are discouraged from joining certain activities. They are told, "This is adult stuff: you're too young. Go and play with your friends." An open educational culture should do its best to avoid discouraging inquisitive youngsters from joining adult activities because even if they tag along and don't quite understand everything going on, they may get a lot out of the experience... and they'll appreciate being included. Afterward, they'll want to go and play with their friends.

An open society is not just open in heart and mind; it is also open physically wherever and whenever possible. With most workshops and factories in the Marketplace and Industrial Park open to view, inquisitive minds will have plenty of productive activities to observe to satisfy their curiosity about the way people work and how things are made. The halls of government will always be open for visitors to witness the proceedings, so they can watch a true democracy in action. Visitors can spend some quality time in the hallowed halls of learning attending workshops and lectures or even signing up for a class.

In an enlightened society, political leaders and journalists will be held to high standards. There will be no tolerance for misinformation, racism or sexism of any flavor. With the light of education shining on all aspects of society, there will be no darkness where ignorance can take root. There will be no misleaders espousing quack theories; because no one will fall for them or have any time to waste on nonsense.

5.–Political Science

Government is inevitable. If you cannot govern your affairs, someone else will govern them for you. *Government* is a dirty word in many circles, yet government is not the problem: *bad government* is the problem. Characterizing government as a "necessary evil," doesn't resolve the quandary either because what is necessary is not necessarily evil. There's no escaping government. Anarchists claim the solution is to get rid of government altogether. Anarchy does not necessarily lead to outright chaos as many claim, yet any complex, systematic way of living is simply not possible without some form of organization.

James Madison famously declared "If men were angels, no government would be necessary." I beg to differ with this notion. The angels Madison was imagining must have been rather stagnant creatures with few needs or ambitions. Holding people's worst impulses in check, as the reference to angels implies, is certainly one function of good government, yet the main purpose of government is to establish a framework for organizing human and natural resources to foster safety, prosperity and well-being.

Most citizens operate with the assumption their governments are providing essential services—principally police, fire fighting, maintenance and elementary education. Residents expect their streets to be clean, their water to be safe to drink and dangerous criminals to be kept behind bars. After all, citizens voted for candidates who promised all good things. Citizens celebrate their government on public holidays watching parades and fireworks displays. They see police cars patrolling the streets and fire fighters protecting their community. They don't expect everything to be perfect, but for the most part they expect things to be on the up and up.

Bad governments resist reform because they don't want to give up their evil ways. Corrupt governments stifle innovation, suppress wages and hinder progress. The corrupt leaders running the show do their best to hide the public funds being siphoned into private pockets. They contrive false justifications for regressive laws and backward policies that benefit their personal wealth and the interests of their patrons.

Bad government is headline news. Good government is rarely talked about. When government does a proper job, citizens pay it little mind and go right to the sports page or entertainment website. Citizens complain about the poorly-paved roads while failing to acknowledge the well-paved roads. News presentations that feature brewing scandals and ongoing disputes leave many with the impression their government is lousy and incompetent. In reality, most governments function pretty well day-to-day, and hardworking public servants receive scant acknowledgement for their dedication and hard work. Good governments do not draw attention to themselves and are pretty boring most of the time. They quietly go about their business so everyone else can go about theirs.

When I was growing up in New York City, I met people who were proud to live in mob-dominated neighborhoods because the mobsters had a reputation for keeping the neighborhood safe. The point is most citizens are willing to tolerate a little corruption as long as it doesn't get out of hand. Sorry to say, it tends to get out of hand. One must wonder why just skimming a little off the top is rarely good enough, but you're not a criminal, so you don't think like a criminal.

When people are troubled by the state of affairs, they look to the political sphere for answers. A fresh crop of idealistic candidates emerges every few years promising better days to come. Voters get their hopes up; yet once the victorious candidates take office, citizens reluctantly realize—once again—that promises of change aren't change. Hope springs eternal until people realize it's the same old story as before with only a few not very significant improvements.

When people become concerned with their government and decide to get involved, their first impulse is to join the good fight for reform. Please consider the alternative of working to establish a new-fangled, private, members-only governing system. Call it as a resource-management system if you prefer. Such an unusual endeavor is not necessarily driven by a sense that one's government is horrible beyond belief or impossible to reform. Maybe it's just more fun and personally satisfying to work with a new thing rather than holding up a sign to change an existing institution. Perhaps pursuing a crazy escapade to improve the world is just what the doctor ordered to get you out of the house, out of your head and introduce you to some fellow idealists.

The best governments are not always the ones that govern least. Often enough, a hands-off approach to a pressing problem is called for because some problems resolve themselves and most organizations work best when they are left to their own devices. At other times, a hands-on approach is called for because most problems do not solve themselves, especially when someone is profiting from the problem in question. It is wholly in the public's interest that dangerous industries are held to high safety standards.

The best governments harness their citizen's intelligence and ambition for the greatest possible creativity, inventiveness and productivity with the least amount of lawlessness, unemployment and sickness. The debate over the size of government misses the point. The important question is whether government agencies are effective. Simply put, good government agencies are the ones that succeed at accomplishing what they were tasked to do.

America can serve as an exemplar for both the best and the worst governments can do. The United States has progressed from slavery and children laboring eighty-hour weeks for subsistence wages to union laborers working forty-hour weeks for good pay and benefits. In every measure of prosperity, health and quality of life, America often scores high, yet in other instances it has scored pretty low such as childhood poverty, income inequality and incarceration rates. America has exhibited a dual personality at times being the kindest, most generous nation on Earth and other times being the cruelest and most inconsiderate.

The model government outlined in this book is designed to truly realize the American ideals of liberty and justice for all of its participants. The private-commonwealth model honors its roots in Classic philosophy, Enlightenment thinking and Judeo-Christian ethics. My proposal is not meant to be a refutation of the American way, but rather an upgrade inspired by a can-do spirit. The purpose of the plan presented in this book is not to prove others wrong, but instead to demonstrate what really works to best serve the people.

A private-commonwealth people's corporation is similar to traditional public governments in several respects. It fulfills all the functions of a traditional government. It is founded on a corporate charter which outlines its purpose, structure and methods. It establishes and maintains the superstructure in which every other organization operates. It sets the rules and procedures, decides on basic policies and settles disputes.

Local government happens when estate residents assemble to discuss their affairs. An open forum is the best way for neighbors to put their minds together. With a fair-minded democratic spirit, governing local affairs can be a lot of fun.

Everyone's personality will be on full display. The clowns in the crowd can lighten the mood if need be. Youngsters will be invited to sit in the circle to get a feel for the governing process. Aside from any pressing matters, governing estate affairs will mostly be about how to spend the discretionary budget and coordinate neighborhood affairs.

In true democracies, there will be differing schools of thought concerning vital issues, yet a dynamic government-by-discussion will discourage a hard divide into bitterly opposing factions. Residents of these future societies will have a thorough understanding of their history and the philosophy behind their way of life, so they will be able to question the principles their way of governing is based upon. A political system able to cultivate its own best critics will be able to reform itself by itself. Rather than waiting for problems to build to a breaking point, wise leaders can identify them early on and deal with them in a timely manner.

Establishing an enlightened government is the precise opposite of forming a criminal organization. Criminals operate in secret and do their best to hide the devious methods they use to make their money and run their operations. Criminal organizations gravitate to an authoritarian, command-and-control power structure whereas true democracies foster an open-and-egalitarian power structure.

Establishing a government that brings out the best in human nature can be likened to harnessing the power of water.

Just like people, water can be both wonderful and horrible. Water gives life and water takes life away. Water has the power to drown, flood and destroy. Over the course of history, humankind has learned how to tame river water with dams, spillways and canals. Roofs and gutters protect buildings from rainwater. People protect themselves against rain with umbrellas and waterproof jackets. In much the same way we have learned how to handle water, the best governments will be able to tame and harness the whimsical desires, wayward intelligences and unpredictable passions of human beings.

6.–Prehistory

Sentimental folks have been longing for a simpler past for as long as there has been a past to long for. Mythologies of prehistoric paradises began in ancient times. The Book of Genesis begins in the Garden of Eden. Greek poets and Roman historians imagined idyllic origins of humankind. The Amazons were a mythical tribe of warrior women who lived beyond the bounds of the civilized world. With the discovery of the Americas, the Old World encountered New World people, and native peoples once again captivated the popular imagination of Europeans. Noble savages became characters in romantic adventure stores. A century later, indigenous peoples became the subject of anthropological inquiry. With the development of photography, the publication of *National Geographic Magazine* (first issue: October, 1888), the general public saw the first photographs of people living outside of the "civilized" world.

Trailblazing anthropologists, beginning as early as the 1850s, set out to live with indigenous peoples with high-minded intentions of "civilizing" them. Contrary to expectations, adventurous anthropologists discovered that despite a lack of modern technology, tribal peoples possessed rich cultures and deep spiritualities. The learning went both ways. While most of the world was busy with war and empire, aboriginal peoples spent the years perfecting how to live in harmony and many of their Golden Ages lasted for generations.

Native peoples have been romanticized, demonized, mythologized and stereotyped; perhaps obscuring the lessons they have to teach. Many original peoples are now preoccupied with conserving their culture while integrating with the modern world and are doing well in protected territories that allow them to preserve their way of life. Their survival against the odds is a living testimony to the wisdom of ancient ways.

To get ahead, let us look back in time to retrieve the valuable things that may have been lost or forgotten along the way. To gain a full sense of any important feature of modern life, it is useful to go back to its origin. Throughout this book, admittedly with some dramatic license, I trace many features of modern living (private property, trade, industry, villages, cities, law) to their prehistoric origins.

Imagining our primitive past evokes a romantic longing for a primeval state living under the stars roaming wild and free. The further back in time one goes, the more difficult it is to get a clear picture of how people lived. Needless to say, there are no chronicles of particular people or events before the advent of writing. Nevertheless, a compelling sense of how prehistoric people lived can be derived by combining the archeological evidence with anthropologists' observations of indigenous peoples living in the modern world. Scientific studies of indigenous people continually evoke a picture of prehistoric human societies more intelligent, creative and dynamic than previously thought.

7.–History

Life on Earth began with stromatolites about 3,500,000,000 years. Geological history goes back 4,500,000,000 years and cosmological history goes back about 13,700,000,000 Earth years. Currently, *history* generally refers to the history of people since writing was invented—hence the term *prehistoric* refers to anything before written records. Even though Homo sapiens have been around for about 250,000 years, human prehistory should be traced through the hominid family tree going back several million years because much knowledge was passed from earlier to later hominid species and finally to our species. The last hominids to go extinct were the Neanderthals about 30,000 years ago in what is now Spain.

The recording of history began with storytelling. Witnesses to notable events were inspired to recount stories and since there was no writing, to commit those stories to memory. Histories were the first stories. Memorabilia preserved personal remembrances. Cemeteries conserved family history. Paintings and drawings interpreted memories. The first songs and poems told stories passed down from generation to generation. Renowned warriors and exalted leaders were romanticized as heroes. The anniversaries of great events were commemorated. Unfortunately, most of the stories and songs committed to memory over many generations are lost to history. History really came alive with writing. Writing began 5,200 years ago with crude market invoices and shipping contracts. The intentional recording, study and analysis of events did not begin until 2,500 years ago with the ancient Greeks: Herodotus, Thucydides, Xenophon. Roman historians continued the tradition: Tacitus, Suetonius, Livy.

Since ancient times, the methods available to record information (hence history) have come a long way. Paper was invented in China around A.D. 105. Before that, most writing was done on expensive animal skins or crude papyrus. In 1440, the first printing presses became available. Before that, all we have are hand-written accounts. The first practical photographic equipment became available in the 1840s. Before that, we only have drawings, paintings, sculptures and written descriptions. Since the invention of motion pictures around 1888, most consequential world events have been captured on moving pictures. The first color motion pictures were released in the late 1930s, yet it took several decades for movies and television to fully transition from black-and-white to color. As computer technology has archived every kind of media over the past half century, more history is recorded more accurately every year.

The great tragedy of history is how people don't learn from history despite the oft-repeated admonition of being condemned to repeat it if we fail to learn its lessons. When history repeats itself, it's like watching the same bad movie over and over again while most people are longing for a new movie with better characters and a plot that makes sense. As far as the big picture of history and current events, people search for insights by identifying historical parallels with past periods when similar issues were being contended with. To divine the next step in human development, it is best to be familiar with the steps that came before it. If you want to make history, it is good to be familiar with history.

The compromises made during the United States Constitutional Convention concerning slavery (the three-fifths compromise, the fugitive slave clause and the debate over slavery in new territories) sowed the seeds of America's most deadly and divisive conflict. The American Civil War erupted seventy-four years after the ratification of the United States Constitution. Founding members should ask themselves how they are possibly sowing the seeds for their own division.

Never put yourself above suspicion as the potential author of your own demise. It is hard to imagine how things can go so wrong so quickly when things are going right. Yet history comes with a warning against sudden failure despite the best of plans. The winds of change have been known to blow unpredictably in the wrong direction. Revolutionaries must ask themselves how they will keep the revolutionary passion burning. How do you ensure succeeding generations will not become lazy and complacent? People forget as memories fade over time. People will let down their guard because the whole point of working hard was to relax and enjoy yourselves. Hence it makes sense to create something to remind future generations to be cognizant of how easily paradise can be lost.

An enlightened society puts all the social sciences to good use. At a private commonwealth's inception, founding members will consult historians and political scientists. Visionary educators will be called upon to help establish state-of-the-art education systems. Renowned economists will be consulted to help design the most self-sufficient and resilient local economies. City designers will draw insight from visionary urban planners to clarify their guiding concepts and refine their designs. Psychologists will enjoy treating a broad spectrum of open-minded and honest patients. Sociologists will observe and treat a whole society receptive to their ideas. Administrators will employ social-science methods to monitor the successes and failures of their policies.

Five

WHAT'S THE PROBLEM?

1.—Waste

After cashing their paycheck, some wage earners can't resist the urge to splurge on good times and fancy things they can barely afford. Come payday, people who worked hard all week gather at the local bar and after all that hard work those cold beers sure taste good. Those cold brews take the edge off, so those first drinks lead to the next round and the next round after that. Money is hard to earn and easy to spend; but come payday, many lose sight of this simple concept. Too many of us are hopelessly attracted to the shiny new things we can buy today but cannot afford over the long run.

International trade is driven by the demand for each nation's unique resources. The most abundant resource in many emerging countries is the cheap labor that produces the inexpensive goods whose sales drive today's mass consumption. International commerce based on inexpensive merchandise wastes a lot of energy. Container ships consume hundreds of thousands of gallons of heavy fuel transporting consumer goods halfway around the world. Semi-trucks burn thousands of gallons of diesel fuel bringing those goods from port to market. Much of this merchandise is soon tossed in the trash. Be that as it may for now, a better way of international trade is on the horizon. As emerging countries develop more efficient industry and infrastructure, much of the world is moving toward an enlightened age of international trade driven more by prosperity and less by poverty.

Once something has gone to waste, there is no getting it back—wasted moments, wasted opportunities, all the waste caused by all the other waste. Waste is a bummer. But we are not here to cry more tears over all the waste in the world today. For various and sundry reasons, a lot of potentially productive time goes to waste in the modern world. More than two million American prison inmates waste their lives away behind steel bars and barbed-wire fences. Billions of hours of precious time are mindlessly squandered staring at the television or noodling on social media. Millions of drivers pound their steering wheels in frustration while crawling through rush-hour traffic. The more time we burn up, the less time there is to be productive or creative. Wasting limited resources taxes the natural environment. Wasting time weakens the economy.

In wealthy countries, there is a profusion of material waste. Usable, repairable, edible stuff that someone else could use, repair or eat is routinely tossed in the trash. Anyone who has gone dumpster-diving knows, firsthand, about all the good stuff that gets thrown away in wealthy countries. Recyclable paper, plastic, glass and metal are tossed in trash cans only to be buried in the local landfill or burned in the municipal incinerator. Thousands of tons of organic matter that could be composted to enrich the soil ends up in the garbage. Inventory your trash the next time you toss it out. There's probably a lot of paper, plastic packaging and junk mail. Generating wealth without wasting resources is the wise thing to do. Wasting is not getting ahead—wasting is falling behind.

Every culture honors the outstanding inventors and artists who shaped and beautified their world. After a long history of waste and pollution, it behooves us to commission the world's most inventive and creative minds to design the least-wasteful human world possible. Planet Earth needs to be thoughtfully managed, not mindlessly squandered. This beautiful masterpiece of a planet is the household humanity shares; and there is some long overdue housework. Despite progressive policies, many industries continue to abuse the natural environment—taking without giving, destroying without restoring, wasting precious resources for no good reason like there is no tomorrow.

The better future is a lean, green and clean economic machine that thrives in balance with the natural environment. The cities envisioned in the final chapter of this book are limited to 10,000 inhabitants. On such a human scale, the people will not need automobiles. People will walk, run, bicycle, roller-skate, skateboard or use sustainable public transportation to get around their private metropolis. The benefits will add up: residents will save money and avoid much of the dangers associated with automobile traffic. They will breathe cleaner air, get more exercise and have more fun getting to where they are going.

Matter matters. We acquire stuff, we use stuff, we throw stuff away. It is prudent to finally make a full accounting of how we handle all the stuff we traffic in to determine the most efficient ways to conserve and recycle resources. Well-made stuff lasts longer and is worth repairing. Much of what is commonly thrown in the trash and hauled to the dump can be creatively reused. For example, when a wooden house is framed, twenty to thirty percent of the lumber usually goes to waste. In the country, good ol' boys burn the scraps to heat their houses. Those small pieces of lumber and plywood can also be used to make small items like toys, boxes, or birdhouses. Sawdust and wood ash are great additions to any compost pile. With efficient recycling and composting systems, we are on our way to achieving the gold standard of a waste-free world.

One of the greatest wastes in human affairs is the time too many people spend idle, inactive and out of the loop. Misfortunate people are disabled for physical, legal, financial, mental and spiritual reasons. Millions of Americans don't contribute in any significant way to the economy, instead they only take from it—doubling the loss to society. Yet, we still prosper despite so many slackers and misfortunates. Imagine the potential strength of a dynamic local economy that harnesses everyone's productive potential.

The greatest waste in human affairs is the time people squander in antagonistic, contentious and bitter relations. Conflict makes life more complicated than it has to be, wastes time and lowers spirits. Enlightened societies strive to reduce pointless conflict by balancing people's competitive drive with a cooperative spirit. When everyone is on the same page focused on solving common problems, they will be able to cultivate a broader understanding of the choices they face as a group. The people can escape from closed, unequal and unconscious ways of relating by actively cultivating open, equal and conscious relationships.

2.–Over-Commercialization

Modern free-market economies produce a vast spectrum of

goods for the consumer and industrial market. If there's a living to be made making a product, service or type of entertainment, you can be certain someone will be earning a living producing it. The wide spectrum of choices available in free-enterprise marketplaces is beneficial to consumers in many ways. Competition widens choices and lowers prices. Inexpensive apparel enables everyone to have a varied wardrobe: an unheard-of luxury a few centuries ago. Affordable automobiles let drivers get around with ease. Inexpensive air travel allows people to travel across the country and around the world. The entertainment industry is relentless. There is no end to the filmed entertainment released on a regular basis. Besides a broad range of television shows, there is a major motion picture released almost weekly. There is a minor motion picture released almost daily.

Unfortunately, the much vaunted and highly celebrated free market has shortcomings. There is no shortage of harmful ways to earn a buck. There are plenty of incentives to exploit workers, pollute the environment or make exaggerated claims to boost profits. Imposter, online-shopping and investment scams abound. We've all had our share of good shopping experiences when we got our money's worth or better. Unfortunately, we've probably had no shortage of bad shopping experiences when we were overcharged or sold defective goods.

Let us consider the historic process of commercialization

by considering the growth of the sports industry over the last 150 years since the National Baseball League was founded in 1876. People play sports to amuse themselves and find an outlet for their competitive nature. Long before sports became big business, players organized teams to compete. Fans gathered to watch the games, and their enthusiasm raised the stakes. As games evolved into fan-supported events, enterprising people discovered their commercial value. At first, the grandstand admission barely covered the costs of putting on the game. The fans came to love the game and adore the great players; and over the decades, as sports leagues developed, players went from being poorly paid amateurs to become highly honored and highly paid professionals. Since the advent of radio and television broadcasting, several professional sports leagues have grown into enormous money-making enterprises.

Music began with folks playing in their spare time to amuse themselves and their neighbors. Music was a personal and community expression to celebrate life and beautify the world. Music has come a long way since its innocent beginnings. Nowadays music is big business. You probably have to pay big bucks to see your favorite musical artists perform.

Professional athletes and entertainers deserve to be properly rewarded so they can continue pursuing their art and playing their sport. It is unfortunate how so much entertainment and sports have become so profit driven. Most fans would prefer less-expensive and less-commercialized sporting and music events where the emphasis is on the game or the performance—not sucking every last dollar out of fans' wallets with astronomical ticket prices, overpriced food and expensive souvenirs.

Many other industries have been compromised by large corporations that have merged into even larger corporations to maximize profits and leverage market power. Some of these consolidations have been referred to with the prefix *big*: big pharma, big agriculture, big finance, big insurance, big law, big tech. Big can be better; but most of the time, big businesses have developed a myriad of clever techniques to reap larger profits by misinforming the public, stifling competition and getting regulations loosened.

Commercialization is not the problem: over-commercialization is the problem. The profit motive is not the problem. Cheating consumers to maximize profits is the problem. An enlightened society strives to establish a free-enterprise system that serves everyone and harms no one. In exploitation-driven production, producers gain at the expense of workers and people are harmed in the process. In cooperation-driven production; everyone wins and no one is harmed, misinformed or shortchanged.

3.–Addiction

Human beings are curious creatures. Prehistoric wanderers who stumbled upon unusual things pondered the possible uses of what they discovered: "Does it smell good?" "Does it taste good?" "What happens when you bang it with a rock?" "Can I smoke it?" Prehistoric proto-scientists experimented with everything promising—plant, animal and mineral—to determine any possible use. We owe a great debt to countless unknown and unnamed people whose discoveries made vital contributions to basic knowledge.

Human behavior is driven by the desire to feel good. There are many natural ways to feel good—the satisfaction of being productive, the joy of discovering intimacy with a special person, the pleasure of being creative, the delight of discovery, the gratifying exhaustion after athletic activity. Although people are always looking for shortcuts, most natural pleasures are the reward of self-disciplined effort. When pursuing pleasure or joy, the brain releases natural chemicals such as dopamine and related neurotransmitters to reward accomplishment. Drowsy people are drawn to go to bed by the pleasant feeling of drifting off to sleep. Disciplined people make sure to get a good night's sleep to feel refreshed in the morning. Ambitious students study hard for the big exam to enjoy the subsequent rewards of good grades.

Healthy people enjoy the buzz of being a good person and the peace of mind of a clear conscience.

Unfortunately, there are many not-so-healthy ways to feel good by overindulging in one or more of the habit-forming substances discovered, cultivated, refined and synthesized over the long history of getting high. They all have one thing in common: they cost money. Indulgers spend billions of dollars every year on legal and illegal psychoactive substances. Downtown, there's a bar on every corner. Convenience stores sell beer, wine and cigarettes. Tens of millions of people smoke cannabis. Millions of others indulge in cocaine or heroin despite their status as "controlled" substances. Although most people are able to enjoy an occasional drink, puff or snort, others are not able to maintain self-control and become habituated to one or several psychoactive substances. The persistent need for that shortcut to feeling good again overrides any rational acknowledgement of the dangers ahead.

Before habituated indulgers realize it, getting high becomes the new normal. As the habit becomes ingrained, their "friend" slowly turns into an enemy. What was first a bargain, carries an ever-bigger price tag. Falling in love was the easy part. Before long, the honeymoon ends, the romance fades and indulgers start having serious problems. They know they need to end the relationship; but they discover that breaking up is indeed very hard to do.

Consuming psychoactive substances is an easy substitute for the natural pleasures that require self-discipline. Mind-altering substances that induce sublime feelings should be luxuries to be enjoyed on special occasions when there is truly something to celebrate. When luxuries become necessities, people become spoiled. Before they know it, they are addicted.

Despite mounting hassles, addicts remain hopelessly dedicated to their substance(s) of choice. What were first medicines have become poisons. What started out as liberators have transformed into imprisoners. Forlorn addicts are lured inside what they believe are heavenly gates only to have the rusty, creaky, moonlit gates slam behind them. There's quite a different view on the inside. The light is gone. Hope is gone. True friendship is gone. Addicts find themselves in a Hell on Earth: lonely, forgotten, hopeless and confused.

Alcohol is not the problem—Alcoholism is the problem. Alcohol is inanimate; it never poured itself down anyone's throat. Drugs are not the problem. Addiction is the problem. Indulgence is not the problem. Overindulgence is the problem. Mind-altering substances become like an old friend people come to depend on to make them feel good. When they just can't live without "that feeling," they're addicted.

Out-of-control addiction has derailed many promising lives, broken apart families and destroyed countless marriages. Friends and relatives suffer on the sidelines while someone they love turns into a zombie. Other than the obvious medical costs of treating addicts and their families, addiction racks up a big legal bill from law enforcement, courts and prisons. Today, over a million convicted drug dealers, users and their accomplices populate American prisons. Hundreds of thousands of addicts enter detox, rehab and intensive-outpatient programs every year. Imagine the vitality and increased productivity societies freed from addiction could bank on. It behooves us to do our very best to solve the tragedy of addiction once and for all.

Addiction is a pervasive problem. The best comprehensive solution to addiction is establishing a vibrant and dynamic society that encourages healthy habits—neither creating a void in the human soul nor easily supplying the drugs or alcohol to fill those voids. When there are job-performance incentives for staying healthy and easy access to every healthy way of feeling good, substance abuse can be brought under control.

Freed from addiction, people will enjoy the natural pleasures of life once again. Liberated from the monetary, psychological and spiritual costs of addiction, the people will live longer and healthier lives. Emancipated from the trap of addiction, people will awaken from their self-absorbed trances and tune into one another's concerns.

4.–Dishonesty

It's impossible to pinpoint when humans first developed vocal symbols to communicate—likely more than 100,000 years ago. For all we know, crude vocal symbols could have begun more than a million years ago. Once the first sound symbols proved useful, languages grew by inventing, modifying or adopting words from other languages. After spoken language was universal, written symbols came into use. The first complete writing system was developed in Mesopotamia around 3200 B.C. A rich heritage of orally transmitted stories gave early literature a strong start. Words were put to music and songs filled the air. Language grants people the power to communicate, cooperate, teach and learn. Many people abuse the power of this great invention by lying for many reasons in many languages.

How have we come to live in such a dishonest world? Why do we lie so much? The true story is never good enough for some people. Life has to be pregnant with suspense and driven by drama like a Hollywood movie which leads to exaggerated storytelling. People lie for many reasons—to sell, cheat, deceive, swindle, misguide or feed their addictions. However, not all reasons are nefarious. Some people on occasion lie to spare another's feelings because it's less uncomfortable than revealing the inconvenient truth. They may lie to hide their weaknesses because they fear ridicule. Whatever the reason, societies lose when too many people play the liar's game.

Falsifiers and deceivers soon lose sight of the bigger picture. Lies and fabricated justifications have become their way of doing business in this world. They disdain the people who challenge their hidden agendas and quickly lose patience with curious people they suspect are beginning to see through their dirty little game. Once liars have bought into the hustler's game, honest people are nowhere in sight. Honest people?—They're the suckers. Ain't no one really honest in this world—Didn't you know?—Haven't you heard? The truth is for losers—so it's better to live in a fantasy. Why work for your money when people are so easy to swindle? That's fun, right? High-plains drifters and no good grifters... seems there's a conman on every street corner waiting for the next sucker to come along.

The truth has a pesky way of escaping the darkness. Lies come to light, sooner or later. Public officials' private affairs erupt in a new scandal on a regular basis. Some may have gotten away with it once, twice, or even a hundred times until they got caught in the act and forced to resign in disgrace. No lecture tours or book deals for you, buddy—You're branded for life–! When you lie, you have to remember two things: your lie and the truth. When you tell the truth, you only have to remember the truth. Honesty stands at the gateway to harmony. Make honesty your friend and guide... please.

The Valley of Peace is a land of honest people. Imagine that. Honest people more easily see through the lies and can enjoy the peace of a clear conscience. The truth is central to any genuine spiritual quest. How can anyone discover the truth if they do not live the truth and speak the truth? Honesty is the great harmonizer. It promotes higher consciousness and keener awareness. Living in an honest world would be a pleasure; yes, indeed but double that satisfaction with the peace of mind only honest societies can enjoy.

Honesty simplifies human affairs. Dishonesty complicates human affairs. Lying wastes precious time. Honesty saves time. The truth is the light, and dishonesty is the darkness in our lives. Liars are haunted by the unknown. They know there is a conscience working behind the darkness. They fear they'll slip up sooner or later, or maybe the person they just lied to knows somehow deep-in-their-gut their story doesn't add up. Maybe liars haven't figured out all the angles. Maybe their unsuspecting victims are starting to figure out their game.

Dishonest societies are setting themselves up for ruin. Honest societies will sustain. People pursuing enlightenment put dishonesty behind them. They come forth to confess their misdeeds. They recalibrate their minds into truth-telling devices. The open and honest pursuit of local harmony and prosperity will not be in vain. The fools will have flown, the hypocrites will be known, and honest people can get down to business for real.

5.–Loneliness

Love is a big word in the English language. Nothing feels better than being in love. Lovers sing songs and wax poetic about newfound love. Lost love has inspired many poignant lamentations. Nothing hurts more than a broken heart. Human beings are social creatures who need love to thrive. Sometimes, our desire for love goes unfulfilled because prejudices, misunderstandings and animosities contaminate human relations and weaken social bonds.

People seem together when seen together, yet they remain apart in many invisible ways. Human beings want love and attention all day long: at home, at work and everywhere in between, but a lack of fulfillment diminishes many lives. In bad cases, the lonely are estranged from their societies. In worse cases, isolated people sink into melancholy, depression and despair. In the worst cases, isolation drives people to kill themselves.

Despite material sufficiency in prosperous societies, widespread emotional deficiency prevails. Much of humankind is suffering from an intimacy-deficit disorder. By remotely controlling each other, people have grown more distant. All kinds of nonsense and misinformation inhibit more enlightened social networks. Class divisions separate. Cliques insulate. Libel, insult and defamation poison human relations. Grudges consume. Exploitation divides. Prejudices alienate. Anger inhibits intimacy. Whatever is *in the way*, enlightened societies strive to get it *out of the way* to relate better.

The desire for love and companionship leads some people astray. The cold-hearted manipulate the lonely. Careful–! Smiling faces don't always tell the truth. Many women appreciate male adoration. Devious men ply false admiration to have their way with them. Heartbroken people are left out in the cold and grow disheartened. Lonely and disturbed, their hearts grow cold, so it becomes ever more difficult to love like before. When people cannot find the companionship they crave, they gravitate to substitutes. Bad friends are better than no friends, I suppose. Social media can keep you company for a while.

You've loved and lost, and you're the better for it. You have it all figured out—and this time, you can't miss. You swear you "won't get fooled again." Then you play the fool again. Is there a doctor in the house who can prescribe a pill to quell this inordinate desire to be loved? To be adored? To be worshipped? To be made to feel wonderful?

A life without intimacy is shallow and hollow. People are closed off from each other. We need to open up to one another. Loneliness is a pervasive problem. Togetherness is the only solution. Conflict has alienated humankind—cultivating harmony can bring people back together again. We need to be both high-minded and pragmatic. We need one another, so we should open up to find one another. How can you mend a broken heart? Through conscious, caring relationships. Let the nonsense end so intimacy can flourish. Let the disharmony end so people can begin forming societies of freethinking, open-hearted, magnanimous people who love one another for real.

Only love can break the chains of hatred that isolate and alienate people. Only love can bring people back home, and love needs a home to flourish. Hatred has shaped the course of history. Love will reshape the course of our history going forward. Peace-seeking pioneers prosper together by loving one another, doing what they love and loving what they do.

What a wonderful world it will be when people establish peaceful societies free from poverty, over-commercialization, waste, addiction, dishonesty and loneliness. Please pardon this saturation-bombing of your sensitive mind with a few of the bewildering problems confronting humankind today. Yet by pioneering solutions to these problems, life can be much greater than you ever imagined or hoped for.

Six

Begin with Business

1.–Work

P rehistoric nomads chased herds of game migrating across the vast landscape of the untamed Earth to feed their people. Armed with flintstone spearheads mounted on straight sticks, with a good hurl, hunters felled their prey in field and forest. Obsidian knives were used to butcher the kill. At their encampment, the tribe savored their freshly caught meal together around the fire. When it came time to get crafty, those stone knives were employed to carve bone needles which were used to sew fur garments with thread made from sinew. As night fell, a glorious star-filled sky shone above as ancient nomads curled up to sleep by the fire to a natural soundtrack of nocturnal animals and insects. Once the feast was over, hunger drove the hunt anew.

Outdoor enthusiasts enjoy hiking through the woods and

camping in the wilderness to escape civilization. It's good to get away for a while, yet before long, weekend warriors look forward to enjoying the creature comforts and conveniences of modern living. Most of us don't miss hunting in lonely forests and roaming though vast mountain-scapes like our distant ancestors. In prehistoric times, people had to work hard just to survive. Nowadays, most people work hard to live well. Unless you are living from a trust fund or have a hidden magic money tree, you have a job and work for a living.

Business news focuses on classy executives managing mighty organizations, flamboyant financiers dominating securities markets and austere economists gathered in fancy conference rooms debating policy. Focusing on the top of the food chain belies the way an economy truly functions. The basic driving force of an economy is not at the top; rather, it is more toward the bottom. (Drum roll please...) The fundamental driving force of an economy is—WORK—both the physical and mental work deployed in every step of making the goods and providing the services people need and desire. A business is a forum to organize work. Money is a medium of exchange for work. An economy is an elaborate work-exchange system. Work is translated into money. We spend our money on goods and services brought to market by other people's work. Conversely, other consumers spend money on what we produce. It only makes sense for workers to get smart.

Working to thrive is the rule no matter where you go. Work is hard to avoid. Begging is work. Living off the dole requires skill. Unless you have a full-time wait staff or caregiver, you have to wake up every morning and find a way to put some clothes on your back and food in your pie-hole. Vagrants can scratch out an existence living off the fat of the land, but it's not a lifestyle to be envied. To put it simply, we choose to work because we are nothing if we have nothing. We do what we have to at work so we can do what we want to do after work.

I've got some bad news for the lazy people in the crowd. In an egalitarian society, everyone works, participates and contributes. Working together is how we come together. Work is at the heart of building a better world, so we must work together well to succeed. As shareholders in a cooperative venture, we will naturally share common concerns. We will all be playing a part in a process greater than ourselves while dealing with parallel issues and concerns. We will all have skin in the same game.

A fellowship of working people with time on their hands can supplement their earnings through a work exchange. It begins with a group of people taking an inventory of who needs work and who needs work done. By making a list of your talents, tools and available time, you can discover every way you can work for each other and with one another.

Work, my friends, and work together well. I don't care if it's a lemonade stand on a hot summer's day—Cash in on Mama's secret recipe. Look in the garage, scope out the basement, search the attic. What tools do you have? What skills can you muster?

Enter the Hall of the Ultimate Truth to weigh the gold of your worth. I know you would rather be a movie star than get caught doing yard work, but for anyone with little money in their pockets, some work is better than no work. More important than the work itself is how well you work together. After work, don't take the money and run. Hang out with your homies for a while and talk about the future. Your crew's after-work discussions can serve many purposes: getting to know one another, coordinating your efforts and plotting a future for your organization.

When you learn to work together well, you will no longer have to work for other people. Welcome to Entrepreneurship 101: a time to learn seminal truths and comprehend eternal lessons. After working together for a significant period of time, you will have plenty of real experiences to talk about rather than a bunch of dumb ideas you read in some book.

2.–Private Property

The wellbeing of the first people roaming in kinship groups

depended on common possessions. The tribe's spears and arrows killed the beasts that were the mainstay of their diet. The tribe's humble tents kept everyone warm. When it was time to move on, hunter-gatherers collected all their belongings. Packing up their camps, wanderers had some tough choices to make about their stuff: what to lug and what to leave behind. Aside from a few amulets and adornments, everything they carried was essential for their survival. Even after people finally settled down and claimed a place to collect what they found or made, their wellbeing still largely depended on what they accomplished together. Over time, that changed when people began to distinguish their private property: individual, family and community. I worked for it—it's mine. We found it—it's ours. Somebody gave it to us—therefore, it's ours. However, if everyone shares it—that makes it community property.

Considering land as private property is a relatively modern concept. Native Americans were bewildered when they first observed European newcomers erecting fences to mark the boundaries between properties. Most natives had a more fluid sense of the land they laid claim to. Semi-nomadic peoples considered the lands they cultivated and traversed to be the commonwealth of their kinfolk, and hoarding land or delineating it with fences was foreign to them.

In many early societies, the number of horses in the family stables was equated with household wealth. The word *equity* is derived from the Latin word for horse. Within imperial realms, slave holdings measured a household's worth. In polygamous tribes, the number of wives reflected a household's wealth. Even today, in some African societies, heads of cattle or numbers of goats are a measure of wealth. The word *capital* is derived from the word *cattle*, and domesticated farm animals are referred to as *livestock*. Nowadays, wealth is defined as net worth: what one owns minus what one owes. Yet wealth is more than property or money in the bank. Wealth is no good if one is no good in getting it, yet wealth can do a lot of good when it is prudently invested in productive resources.

Shipwrecked on a deserted island, in the aftermath of a hurricane enduring hard times; survivors naturally come together to share what little they have. Once there's a surplus, some people gain more than others and the squabbling over resources begins. A central challenge of an egalitarian business system is stakeholders discovering how to share their economic pie so everyone is satisfied with their slice. Fortunately, in an egalitarian society, the aim of each shareholder's wealth (staying healthy, prosperous and well-educated) becomes the source of their wealth creating a positive feedback loop encouraging wisdom, health and prosperity. A level playing field encouraging fair competition should grant each of us a realistic self-perception. We will be encouraged to develop our strengths as well as accept our shortcomings. The pleasure of sharing will overcome any impulse to hoard. The joy of cooperating will overcome any desire to dominate.

3.–Invest in Local Harmony

Prudent investors buy what they believe to be undervalued stocks. Then they do their best to sell their overvalued securities just before the price begins to fall. Investors rarely know exactly how their money is being used. Gazing down upon the world from their fancy office suites, high-powered professional investors, whose attentions are fixated on the bottom line, are worlds away from the people and natural environments their wheeling and dealing are affecting.

Your trusted investment advisor calls with a hot lead—Great news–! The Acme Mining Company has set up shop in Botswana on a fresh claim, and preliminary core samples are showing great promise. With an infusion of capital, they can go for the mother lode. How much are you willing to wager? You consider investing. Rumors are circulating that it's the find of the decade. Maybe miners will uncover immense underground caverns of diamonds and gold and your stocks will explode. Maybe not. Glossy brochures featuring photographs and fancy charts are all you have to go by. Botswana is half a world away, so there's no way you can know exactly what is happening. Will they exploit the local people? Will your gain come at the expense of the natural environment? Will the venerated Acme Mining Company create a dangerous mess? Does your investment come with an iron-clad assurance there won't be any funny business? Situated so far away, will they hide the find and defraud you of your fair share? And if they do hit pay dirt, will they compensate you fairly. Will you ever know? Can you ever know?

When you invest in your own local business system, you will know precisely where your money is going and how it is being used. You will be directly investing your time and talent in the enterprise system you own a stake in. Your money will fuel your own local system's growth. No one will be able to hoard any part of your wealth or earn excessive profits from your hard work. There will be no extravagant C.E.O.s, C.F.O.s or fat cats skimming money to buy Lear jets to fly to their private islands at your expense.

If you are searching for a better way to prosper, I recommend going into business—not for love of money—rather to earn your living doing something you love. Put your minds together, not above and below one another. Strive to become the most productive, creative and reliable practitioners of your craft or profession. Concentrate on mastering your craft rather than mastering being crafty. After all is said and done, integrity is the surest way to win customer loyalty and gain market share over the long run. While your competitors are bragging in their silly ads how incomparably great they are, your company will be the best for real.

Each person's professional reputation in the community and their ability to earn a better living will depend on doing work people are happy with. Word on the street has got to be that you're good at what you do, or you just won't be able to get ahead. If you hope to hold your head high in our town, you'll also have to fess up to your mistakes.

Aspiring entrepreneurs are well-advised to choose their collaborators carefully. Prospective partners should take note of their differences. Does it feel like a glorious future awaits, or is there something that doesn't feel quite right about the proposed arrangement? Ask around. Then ask yourself if your partners' idiosyncrasies will eventually drive you apart. Sleep on it. Someone walking through the door may be an odd fellow, yet they may very well be a great team player. One can work with an oddball, while weirdos and assholes are something to avoid altogether.

Prospective business partners should breach the sacred topics of religion and politics. We should talk about our beliefs, faiths and doubts concerning every issue related to going into business together. Getting things started is both the longest and the hardest part yet establishing new businesses should get easier and faster once a small cluster of profitable companies are up and running.

As novice entrepreneurs, you must be realistic about the businesses you try to compete against. You must be level-headed enough to distinguish a distinct opportunity from a losing proposition. Investigate your competitors and carefully weigh the potential of each venture you consider. Learn all you can about your local markets and search for the least expensive ways to test market your ideas.

Your startup company will need a competitive advantage or at least an equal footing to succeed. You can only prosper by delivering goods of a higher quality or at a lower price; or by providing better service or offering greater convenience. By selling good goods and providing good service, your budding enterprise will earn the goodwill of your customers. Satisfied customers will then provide the best and least expensive form of advertising: positive word-of-mouth referrals and glowing personal recommendations.

4.–Begin with Business

We begin with business because some degree of prosperity is necessary to pursue personal, social and political harmony. We begin with business because it is easier to rearrange capital and human resources than to rearrange families or forge a new political order. Grand visions of a glorious future must begin with small, local, practical visions. By steady earning, consistent learning, prudent investing and dynamically diversifying into new ventures, your business system will grow. Newcomers in search of opportunity will be attracted to join your growing enterprise system with their tools, talents, connections and experience.

The people's corporation is the bigger organization that fosters the birth of many smaller organizations with tender care and finesse. A savvy enterprise system is especially careful to avoid squandering capital on failing ventures. The pathways to profitability are constantly shifting in this ever-changing world of advancing technology, limited resources and changing tastes. Entrepreneurs who take risks and succeed are hailed as heroes while losers are left choking in the dust. We understand that risk is necessary; yet as part of a people's corporation, we must carefully gauge our risks, learn our lessons fast and cut our losses quickly.

An entrepreneur's worst nightmare is a failing business. Few things are harder than letting go of a broken dream. Obsessed entrepreneurs nursing failing businesses find it nearly impossible to stop spending all their time and money on an enterprise they've poured their blood, sweat and tears into making a success. Heartache after heartache—it's impossible to let go. Even after borrowing as much as they can, mortgaging the house, sleeping in the store, eating at the soup kitchen and taking it to the limit with every credit card they can get their hands on, they just cannot give up their heart-wrenching struggle until the sheriff shows up to repossess the property. Business failures ruin lives—almost as bad as losing a loved one. It is nearly impossible for losers who fight to the bitter end to get ahead again. Forget about a comfortable retirement. A failed entrepreneur will need to work till their dying day just to pay off their debts. Our people's corporation will not let such entrepreneurial oblivion happen.

By all means draw inspiration from large-scale industry but scale down your vision a few clicks. Your small startup will not be able to compete against the big guys. You won't be able to fabricate tires, mine minerals or mill fabrics. You would be able to service and retread tires, smelt iron and aluminum in small furnaces and design and manufacture clothing with fabrics made by the large mills.

Welcome to our Entrepreneurs' Circle. You and your fellow entrepreneurs begin by making a list of skills, resources and ideas for prospective companies. Then continue by putting forth propositions and brainstorming business plans. If mothers lament how difficult it is to find good daycare for their toddlers, ponder what it would take to start a conscientious, caring, daycare center. Aspiring daycare impresarios will be dealing with the same local market as any other daycare entrepreneurs in your town, so you must make a diligent search for every way to throw some magic into your mix so the fledgling enterprise really takes off. A lively private-commonwealth estate with several mothers already looking after their own toddlers could provide a distinct advantage for a daycare venture. To form a strong fellowship, you should sit down after work to have a short discussion about your workday to explore every way you can work better together. If a dreamy mood overcomes the crew, you can use that opportunity to discuss the future prospects of your enterprise. In the beginning, experiment with various ways of working together. Take the time to discover who you like to work with before you commit yourselves to a more permanent arrangement.

5.–Private-Commonwealth Company

Once primitive hunting parties had cornered their prey after a long chase, the tribe certainly wanted their best spearman making the final throw. Long ago, people discovered how things turn out better when each member of the team does what they do best. Lo and behold—specialization leads to better outcomes and increases productivity. Specialization also widens the variety of what is produced. Settling down spurred ever-greater specialization as each family in the village gravitated toward a craft (e.g. stonework, leatherwork, pottery, weaving, beadwork, needlework, etc.).

When crafty people began trading their wares with one another, the first market economies came into being. Many families adopted the name of their trade: baker, smith, carpenter, gardener. Over the course of history, family businesses evolved into large-scale factories, but modern industry lost many of the advantages of family businesses. Family businesses also fell out of favor because most children exposed to a wide choice of possible career paths are not inspired to follow in the narrow path of their parent's footsteps. Private-commonwealth companies return to organizing in small, tight-knit groups dedicated to a particular trade. These voluntary organizations bring back the intimacy of family businesses while bypassing the drama and inflexibility of working with family members.

Private-commonwealth companies are the basic unit of for-profit and not-for-profit businesses that comprise a people's corporation. All paid work is done, and all income is earned by companies. Formal teaching is provided by education companies. Medical care is performed by healthcare companies. Retail manufacturing is done by Marketplace companies. Private-commonwealth companies are employee-owned and managed, so workers are both managers and laborers. The advantages of employee ownership are stable employment in a steady career, workers determining the quality of their work life and sharing the profits. The disadvantages are a loss of free agency, a decrease in wages when profits decrease and difficulty letting go of underperforming workers.

Private-commonwealth companies can be likened to sports teams because they employ a limited set of players.

Sports teams form companies to purchase equipment, contribute to the maintenance of facilities and compete in a league. Baseball teams field nine players. Basketball teams send five players to the court. Football teams put eleven players on the field. Each sports team's goal is to win. A sports team cannot increase their chances of winning by putting more players on the field. They can only increase their chances of winning by fielding better players who coalesce into a great team.

Everything beautiful, except the Universe itself, exists within limits. Would a rose be more of a rose if it were bigger? The greatest of paintings, no matter how much they fill our visual imagination, are limited to the size of their canvases. Movies, even when they successfully transport us to boundless worlds, are limited to their picture-frame and timeframe. The greatest singers are limited to their vocal range. Our life on Earth is limited by the physical and mental capacities of our mortal bodies as we grow up and then grow old.

Private-commonwealth companies are limited to ten principal owner-shareholders. Limiting the number of owner-employees in a business organization keeps the human element simple. Limited organizations conserve the small-group consciousness that enables stakeholders to relate openly and equally. Like a sports team, once a company has grown to its limits, the incentive is not to get bigger, but to get better at what they do. A limited company is also like a sports team because they train auxiliary players and are part of an organized league of companies. Much the same way teams organized in leagues are precisely compared, companies can be accurately compared for productivity, sales, employee satisfaction, customer satisfaction and last but certainly not least—profits.

The short list of possible private-commonwealth companies runs a hundred or more. The long list... up to a thousand. How about opening the best ice cream factory-parlor on the planet? Agriculture appeals to some, so living on a farm is their ideal. For many frustrated motorheads, commonwealth automotive conglomerates will be their power spot. Computer skills? Are you kidding? And the list goes on to pretty much cover the set of businesses one would find in any small city; trade companies: carpenters, plumbers and seamstresses; professional companies: doctors, lawyers, dentists, accountants; and retail companies of every common and many uncommon sorts.

When a private-commonwealth company reaches the limits of its growth, it diversifies into two companies. When a general clothing company reaches its limits, it diversifies into a men's and a women's clothing company located right next door or across the street from each other. When the men's and women's clothing companies reach their limits, they further diversify into a wide variety of apparel categories such as casual, formal, dancewear, sportswear, leather, lingerie, etc. Such a conglomerate of companies cooperates in every possible way by sharing resources and maintaining close cooperative ties.

Businesses are like crystals. Each has many facets. In a private-commonwealth company, every member is involved in every facet of the business. Every worker is a doer, a thinker and a creator: both a generalist and a specialist. Every owner participates in the management of the organization from their first day to their last. Limiting the size of private-commonwealth companies is a rigid rule, yet the tradeoffs are well worth the stability and variety created by a diverse series of equally sized small companies. Each new company will add to the ecosystem of the people's corporation by fortifying its system of established companies.

Private-commonwealth companies grow by producing more and better products rather than more of the same product. A growing and diversifying marketplace of private-commonwealth companies will be able to offer an increasingly wider variety of high-quality, locally-produced merchandise, services and recreation enriching an increasingly self-sufficient local economy. Picture yourself working in a diversified, vibrant, pulsating complex of cooperating companies with daringly creative shops and sumptuous restaurants. Sounds better than another ho-hum day at the office or tedious shift at the factory.

Amalgamations of private-commonwealth companies can

work together in several ways. Like the building trades, a general contractor can hire a set of subcontractors to get complex projects done. For manufacturing complicated products, a series of companies can form an assembly line, each company performing a distinct set of steps in the manufacturing process. In a private-commonwealth university, each department is an education company. The collaborative effort of making a movie is accomplished by a series of companies: the acting company, the production company, the special-effects company, the makeup company, the costume company, the marketing company. A food conglomerate would be composed of a full range of companies: growers, grocers, processors, bakeries and restaurants. A general hospital would be composed of a series of independent medical companies each dedicated to a specialty.

It is vogue to characterize expanding organizations as developing *organically*, which is just a newer, hipper way of saying *naturally*. A growing company in our community begins their day with a morning meeting. Members who sleep on their worries are liable to hatch new ideas, and it's best to express ideas when they're fresh so they can contribute to the ongoing brainstorming process. After a fruitful early-morning discussion, the crew gets to work. No matter how organic or natural their approach, a company grows by getting better at what it does. Many workdays will end with a debriefing to discuss the accomplishments of the day and the challenges of tomorrow. Then, at the end of the week, company representatives bring their concerns and inspirations to their league meetings.

In most manufacturing companies, the thinkers work separately from the doers. In a large furniture company, the design department is found in a cool, high-ceilinged, tall-windowed suite of rooms full of neatly dressed, ever-so polite people, far removed from where their designs are produced. Meanwhile back on the windowless factory floor, not-so-clean-or-well-mannered craftspeople and technicians do their work remote from the creative process and have little say in the design of what they produce or in the management of the business. If the "big guys" upstairs manage things poorly, line workers can lose their jobs regardless of their dedication or performance.

Managers determine the quality of work life of their employees. Some conscientious managers go out of their way to make work as congenial as possible. Yet all too often, there is little incentive for managers to do anything but the minimum. Some spiteful managers relish making their workers as miserable as possible. At the opposite extreme are the luxurious work environments where no expense is spared to create a fun and healthy place to work. Private-commonwealth company partners do their best to create the most attractive working facility possible *within their means*. Imagine large windows flooding the workshop and retail store with sunlight; and in the back, a clubhouse centered around the main office continuing with a simple kitchen / conference room-dining area / nap room / a small backyard—maybe even a company dog.

Forging a strong fellowship is the first challenge in forming a private-commonwealth company. Your fledgling company's initial discussions may prove challenging, yet they should be well worth it over the long haul. The freewheeling discussion is the antidote to the communication breakdown between co-workers. The purpose of company discussions is for workers to gain an awareness of how their behaviors are affecting productivity and the overall spirit and mood. The purpose of advanced entrepreneurial discussions is to develop a master investment scheme. Time to start scheming.

6.—The Art of the Discussion

The fire was at the center of ancient encampments. Firelight beckoned nighttime wanderers home. The fire kept wild animals at bay. Meals were cooked, decisions were made, ideas were discussed and disputes were settled around the fire. Since people learned how to start fires, campers have sat around the flames to enjoy their warmth and light. They also enjoyed the warmth radiating from the people glowing in the firelight. Fortunately, one does not have to build a fire to sit in a circle.

Sitting in a circle is the best way for a small gathering of people to relate in the fullest possible way. Sitting in a circle is a symbol of openness—there is no one to hide behind. A circle is a symbol of oneness—no one has a superior position. Sitting in a circle is a symbol of equality—everyone is the same distance from the middle. A circle is a symbol of completion—the circuit is closed. A revolution is one turn of a circle. The center of a circle of people represents the fire within each person.

In most formal assemblies, people sit in a rectangular arrangement. Students face the teacher in a classroom, pews face the pulpit in a church, the court faces the judge in a courtroom, theater audiences face the performers on stage. In a rectangular arrangement, people form a broadcast network of communication. Holding a discussion with most people facing forward necessitates a lot of neck-craning and head-bobbing. Rectangular arrangements are appropriate for lectures, performances and presentations. An audience cannot watch a movie sitting in a circle.

A circular seating arrangement enables more interpersonal connections. If ten people are relating in a broadcast arrangement, one person addresses nine other people; so at most there are nine one-way relationships. If ten people sit in a circle and relate in a network, each person relates to nine other people, so that's ninety (10×9) two-way relationships. When it's time to listen to a lecture or watch a play, sit facing the stage. When it's time to get down to business with one another, arrange yourselves in a circle.

Lively discussions will activate your imaginations, exercise your brain-muscles and arouse your passions. When we sit in a circle with our fellows, we should prepare to be stimulated. Prepare to be challenged. Speak your minds. Share your hearts. Warm up to one another. Talk about everything you want to talk about but always keep the business plan uppermost in mind. Strive to organize with a heart to create an organization with heart. The name of the new game is—*fair play*. Come clean, put your cards on the table to devise a winning strategy working together.

Most importantly, let go of the need to be the center of attention. You probably speak well, but to be successful, you must learn to listen well. You don't have to be right all the time, or be in charge of everyone. Please let go of any cherished notion that you are oh-so-smart beyond belief. You must realize that you can accomplish much more collectively, and working together will in no way compromise your individuality or inhibit the full use of your talents.

Dreamers relish devising grand schemes. Deep thinkers enjoy elucidating astute observations. Brilliant minds take pride pontificating profound principles. There are appropriate times to ascend the lofty heights of the infinite generativity of the human intellect and imagination. At times, you should let yourselves climb the clouds in your minds and get caught up in the moment as fancy takes flight. Yet dramatic dreamers and inspired visionaries must know when it's time to come back down to Earth. Profound diversions are enlightening and uplifting, but fleeting emotions of fascination and wonder wear off pretty quickly. We must not lose sight of the primary objective of building the better economic machine *today* that will give us lasting satisfaction *tomorrow*.

If the crowd is rowdy, a humble host may need to facilitate a discussion amongst an unruly gathering of misanthropes. A brief dictatorship might be the best way to prime the pump if the mood is overly rambunctious. Okay; look... it's better than everyone going home. Like a teacher in a classroom, the moderator calls on people who raise their hands to keep the discussion moving forward in an orderly fashion.

In several Native American traditions, whoever is speaking holds a feather while they talk. After introducing yourselves to one another, it's time to break out the feather. Once the person speaking is finished, they pass the feather (or another designated object) to the next person in the circle. The magic feather is eventually passed to you. Everyone else's eyes are now on you. You're catching a vibe. Like it or not—it's your moment in the spotlight. You have a choice—monologue, moderate or open things up by inviting your fellows to speak freely.

When the feather is passed to me, if there are no pressing

issues and the mood is relaxed, I'll open the floor before I begin my eloquent oration. I give my friends license to interrupt me to keep the discussion as lively as possible. Under most circumstances, I'm not bothered by interruptions, rather I'm inspired. Now my compatriots won't have to hold onto their thoughts anxiously awaiting their turn to express themselves rather than paying attention to me. I start talking, someone interjects, I reply, someone else has something to say, the open discussion takes flight and many minds unify. I become the conductor of an orchestra of minds, aiming to pull out the best ideas. It is of little importance whose mind the next idea happens to pop into. We're mutually inspiring one another to harvest the best ideas. Fighting over credit is a waste of time.

Our compatriots will naturally loosen up as the discussion progresses. Levity will raise the mood—a few laughs lighten things up. Don't bother taking notes, rather concentrate on listening well. Be considerate and do your best to be succinct. As the evening wears on, bodies feel pleasantly tired, yet minds remain fully awake. Ideas long forgotten suddenly come to mind. One vision inspires another, and soon we arrive at a common vision. The circle discovers a rhythm. Everyone's pistons are firing in order. The discussion finds a tempo and people are speaking clearly, listening attentively and interjecting smoothly.

Don't mentally rehearse your upcoming brilliant oration.

Often someone else expresses what you had in mind, so you're constantly recomposing all the impressive things *you* are planning to say rather than fully paying attention to what *others* are saying. Some people who are just not getting anything out of it will stand up and leave. Naysayers will have their say and then be on their way.

The ultimate success of an extended discussion depends on the spirit of the revolutionaries gathered in your circle. Positive, magnanimous, big-spirited people are a lot more fun to talk with than argumentative idiots. Spend more time looking forward than looking back. Master the art of the discussion to gain your good fortune. When we let go of all of our tensions, pretensions and inhibitions, we can accomplish so much more. As the evening wears on, many people will have spoken their minds about their immediate concerns. The people on a tight schedule will have gone home. Eventually our circle will let go of all formalities and constraints. Hopefully nothing will go awry, but you never know what can happen in this crazy world we live in.

ZoMbIeS roam the night. LoSt sOuLs from tHe Lu-NaTiC fRiNgE may come knocking at the door. There are a lot of nut-jobs out there who have nothing better to do than rant and rave all night long. Difficult people present a challenge. A gathering of peaceful entrepreneurs is most likely a bunch of good folks who don't want to yell and scream or strong-arm anyone, yet all it takes is one sadistic sociopath or conspiracy-nut to walk through that open door and disrupt a peaceful discussion.

Mayhem is not likely. Bad people are not attracted to the company of good people. Dumb people don't like smart people. People without scruples are not interested in goodness. Devious people strive to become experts at appearing to be good, not actually being good. Peaceful pioneers are taking off their masks, not masquerading behind them. The purpose of holding discussions is to cultivate consciousness, not to hone bullshitting skills. Some people will make such fools of themselves they will never come back and blame their embarrassment on good people for the rest of their lives. So be it.

You recall all the times you did your darndest to get ahead, but there always seemed to be something holding you back. You wonder in frustration about everything getting in the way of your success. At the same time, you realize you can't expect your fellows to help you if you don't help them. Please remember that one of the main purposes of forging a strong fellowship is to tap into the power of love. Challenge yourselves to be bold to love. Resolve to choose to love rather than passing quick judgment and banishing the next lost soul who wants to join to the garbage dump of life. How is love going to win unless it is harnessed by those who cultivate its power through love and compassion? Summon the latent powers within. Unleash yourself from what has been holding you back. Do the most beautiful thing you can do. Be the most beautiful person you can be. Time has come for a reckoning. We cannot move forward if we harden our hearts once again. We can only move forward if we open our hearts.

Intimate gatherings have a built-in therapeutic value. Some of us may endure these challenging, never-ending discussions in the hopes of some healing. While digging through the soil of one another's minds, you might come across an unexploded landmine. Careful–! Dealing with painful memories may require delicate psychic surgery. When unpleasant matters come to the surface, go easy and approach the situation gently. Psychic wounds are traumatic incidents that continue to haunt souls, yet when painful issues are revealed and discussed in a loving way, we can bring about real healing. Troubles that haunt people are like big rubber-bands pulling hapless victims back into the pit of past regrets. Let's cut the bands and spring forward rather than being pulled back into the clutches of the wicked ribbons that bound us.

Take the clock off the wall and turn off your cellphones. Awakening the imagination gives a psychosomatic stimulus that animates an active mind in a tired body. Mine your minds. Coffee, anyone? You've covered a lot of ground, and you still have a lot to uncover. Happy digging. You can only master the art of the discussion by learning the lessons it has to teach. You cannot learn this art from a textbook. You can only learn it by doing it. Check it out; the sun is starting to come up. Breakfast, anyone?

Seven

Come Together

1.–The Hippies

The summer of 1967 was heralded as the Summer of Love; and for a brief season, San Francisco was the epicenter of a worldwide party. Despite dire warnings from elders and authorities of every sort, throngs of young people packed their belongings into their station-wagons and V.W. microbuses and hit the road. Proudly wearing tie-dyes, bell-bottoms and dirty red bandanas, they fled their "square" parents to head west, believing better lives awaited them over the next horizon. Worn traditions would be cast aside and replaced by a new culture freed from the constraints of the old. With the open road ahead and blues skies above; Jimi Hendrix, Janis Joplin and the Jefferson Airplane provided an inspiring soundtrack for many grand adventures.

The 1960s were a freer and safer time in America. Wayfarers could pull off the highway into a strange town, scope out some fellow hippies, cop a bag of weed and hook into the local scene. It was easy to make friends and find a crash pad for the night. Thousands ventured in search of a utopian dream that was only partially realized by a fortunate few. To dream, to hope, to explore became a way of life for many searching souls. It was fun to meet the newly enlightened in the American heartland. The most ambitious wanderers longed to meet the movement's royalty. They sought the transcendental golden gateway to Shangri-La and made the Pacific coast of California their ultimate destination that summer.

Much to the consternation of the longtime residents of the Haight Ashbury District of San Francisco, the first hippies on the scene, settled in and got the party started. An explosion of psychedelic art colored the city. There were beautiful, friendly people popping up everywhere. Where Haight Street ends, the majestic Golden Gate Park begins. A three-mile walk west past Hippie Hill winds through eucalyptus, pine and cypress forests, past a carousel, a Japanese tea garden and an arboretum ending at the Coast Highway. Across the highway, the beach and the Pacific Ocean provide an inviting place to lounge in the sand and watch the sun set into the ocean.

The Summer of Love attracted worldwide attention. Major news outlets followed the odd behavior and strange culture of these colorful and freethinking people. If the news media intended to showcase how silly and dangerous hippie life was, their efforts most certainly backfired. It was an attractive lifestyle for teenagers—tune-in, turn-on, drop-out, dress the way you want to dress, think the way you want to think, do plenty of drugs, have lots of sex and go to wild parties and killer concerts forever.

Bohemian enclaves imitating the Haight Ashbury sprang to life in hundreds of cities around the world. For a brief moment, idealists believed the world would come to its senses and magically transform. Many hippies experienced a personal spiritual awakening, yet despite the best of intentions and the most earnest desires, the power structure held sway.

The great Woodstock Music Festival and Harlem Cultural Festival held in the summer of 1969 were music festivals never to be equaled marking the end of a decade never to be equaled. It was a magical time for many, but it could only last for so long. By the mid-'70s, the party petered out and rebellion had lost its luster. Hippie men started cutting off their long hair, their symbol of youthful rebellion, as a rite of passage into adult conformity.

The center of the bohemian universe moved to New York City's Greenwich Village and Lower East Side. Although a collective consciousness and its potential had been felt by many, no one figured out a way to sustain what they'd stumbled upon— tHe DoOrS oF PeRcEpTiOn had briefly opened, then quickly closed. The hippie heyday ended, but the dream never died. For the hippies who wanted to keep the torch burning, the next step was escaping the city.

Disenchanted with the "rat race" in the "concrete jungle" of the big cities and the banality of suburbia; in the early 1970s, many hardcore hippies dropped out to pursue their ideals in the country. Rustic pioneers established remote communities in Oregon, Tennessee, northern California and upstate New York. This Back-to-the-Land Movement spawned many experimental social and economic arrangements: communes, collectives and intentional communities. These idealists did their best to pioneer more harmonious and egalitarian ways of living. Most of these attempts at utopia fell apart after a few years, and only a few of the original communities have survived into the present day.

2.–Bringing Back the Village

More than 10,000 years ago, the first settlers made homes in fertile regions suitable for growing crops and raising livestock. Not having to carry all your possessions was a great leap forward for humankind. Now people could accumulate what they found and gathered. Within an enclosed and secure space, residents didn't have to keep looking over their shoulder or constantly worry about where their next meal was coming from. They had more time to develop their growing village to suit their evolving needs. Settled living inspired many innovations beginning with building the first permanent shelters, fences and furniture. With time to tinker, village dwellers crafted ever better tools and useful household implements.

Huts made with wood and thatch are flammable, so when fires were started, they had to be kept away from nearby dwellings. The fire pit created a central gathering spot. People made good use of the necessary space around the fire pit, which came to serve as the village square. When villagers needed a break, they gravitated toward the fire pit: fire or not. The circular space in the center of the village became a place for celebrations and ceremonies. Trading posts in one corner of the village square were not uncommon.

Early agriculturalists retained many of their wandering ways. While crops grew, men and older boys ventured out on extended hunting expeditions. Women stayed home to tend the homestead and take care of the children. When the men returned from the hunt, the whole village celebrated. After butchering, prepping and roasting choice cuts on the fire, everyone ate together. The village celebrated not just the hunt, but the harvest and the rites of passage into manhood and womanhood. Ancient peoples pounded on drums fashioned from hollow logs covered with animal hides and blew into hand-made flutes as they danced around the fire. When someone demonstrated a natural talent for a certain task, it was delegated to them. Each village revered a medicine man or woman who tended the sick. In village workshops, the trades developed as artisans became more specialized and grew more sophisticated.

Villages grew apace with how much food they were able to produce, and trade expanded with the improvement of roads and the development of more efficient transportation. In medieval times, a majority of the people lived in farming villages organized around a manor. Peasant life was centered around the village church ministered by a village priest. Villages were highly self-sufficient domains hosting a village blacksmith, village baker, tanner and miller. Under a feudal system, serfs were bound to the land and required to pay rent to the lord of the manor.

The first European settlements on North American shores began as villages. A few of the original villages: New Amsterdam, Boston, Philadelphia and Charleston, grew into major metropoles. As more people settled the countryside, villages were established at regular intervals of every fifteen or twenty miles and served as the commercial hubs and cultural centers of agricultural communities. The villages in the most strategically vital locations grew into regional hubs of business and transportation. Nearby villages became satellites of the centrally located cities. Over time, metropolitan areas grew to incorporate nearby villages.

It has become a byword in modern discourse that "It takes a village to raise a child." Take note of how this resonant idea refers to a vague, ephemeral idea of community with no notion of where to find or how to form a village. Drive along the coast, search the dales and glens of the hill country, zoom across farm country, search high and low and what you will discover is the traditional village of our romantic imaginations is nowhere to be found. If it is impossible to find the village of our dreams, the only option is to create that village.

3.–Estate Design

Thousands of fancy condos in hotspot cities such as Dubai, Vancouver, Singapore, London, Miami and New York are purchased by the smart money, sight unseen, and no one ever moves in. So they sit... beautiful places to live with no one living in them; just another asset in an investment portfolio alongside stocks and bonds. Unfortunately, cities with too many ghost apartments cannot thrive. Ghost-apartment dwellers don't eat in the local restaurants. Ghosts don't have children. Ghosts don't form communities. Only flesh-and-blood human beings can form communities.

A private-commonwealth estate is an up-to-date village designed for the modern world. The residents design their neighborhood and choose their neighbors. Living together and sharing expenses decreases the cost of living. Creating a tranquil and rich home environment for people of all ages increases the quality of living. Togetherness makes life fun and easy. Sharing is the simplest way to save time and money.

A private-commonwealth estate is an investment scheme for better living—a monetary investment, a social investment and a spiritual investment. Estate developers pool their resources to establish independent estates in the city, out in the suburbs and way out in the country. Each estate pioneers its own local culture with its own special flavor. What's your flavor? A swank urban apartment building? A spacious suburban campus? A pristine mountain retreat? Estate pioneers scope out properties, compose drawings and crunch numbers to assemble a comprehensive plan for the special lives they want to live. Each estate composes a charter and writes the rulebook for the distinct way of living they envision.

The financial structure of a private-commonwealth estate is similar to a condominium apartment building. Consider this rough estimate: If four people live in a house valued at $400,000, each person's share equals $100,000. Let's say one hundred people living in similar houses sold those homes and pooled their money to build an estate: That adds up to $10,000,000. A band of pioneers would be able to build quite a palace for that kind of money. With their budget in mind, estate designers brainstorm designs for their dream home including private living quarters as well as the common gathering areas, workshops, game rooms; and if they have the real estate, they can add multi-use athletic fields, basketball and pickleball courts.

By exploring distinct architectural expressions, apartment-estate pioneers could develop comfortable urban dwellings by building from the ground up or remodeling defunct hotels, schools and factory buildings. Suburban-estate pioneers develop sunny courtyard apartment buildings and host roadside businesses. Rural-estate pioneers develop remote mountain resorts, academies, monasteries and rehabilitation centers. Rural-estate pioneers with agriculture on their mind can reinvent the family farm, which has been so rudely supplanted by industrialized agriculture. I present a detailed plan in the final section of Chapter Nine: *Estate Design: 7.—Bringing Back the Family Farm*

Private-commonwealth estates conserve the intimacy of nuclear families while enriching growing families with the fellowship of a supportive family-friendly community. Parents will never have to hire a babysitter; there will always be someone around to look after the kids. Village communities will share the burdens, duties and joys of parenthood, pioneering better ways to raise children in the modern world. With a broad spectrum of adult supervision, children will have plenty of elders to seek out for support in every situation, lessening the burden on parents and enriching the social environment throughout.

Welcome to the village. Check out the swank community barbeque pit where villagers are chillin' and grillin.' Smells good: Don't you think? You hungry? Fix yourself a sandwich if you like. Don't miss the next showing at the village movie theatre. They schedule a movie and set aside some time to discuss it afterward. Residents pool their money to build facilities the whole village can enjoy. It's much easier for an organized neighborhood of one hundred people to finance a swimming pool than a single family, and with one hundred or more people living close by, the neighborhood will get much more use out of it. By developing the proper facilities, estate residents will be able to enjoy many types of recreation and pursue a wide range of hobbies. In community workshops, neighbors can share their works in progress with their village-mates for guidance and inspiration. In a playful mood? Did I forget to mention the game room? In a studious mood? Head to the community learning center. Tonight and every night: food, arts and crafts in the heart of a lively village. On special nights—music. On extra-special nights—storytelling and drama.

When villagers are there for one another in their hours of darkness, there will be more love in the light. Villagers come together in good times, yet close-knit neighbors will be there for one another at all times. Set up the *upset station*. With an empathetic elder in the house, distressed people can find the consolation they need in times of trouble. Immediate attention to matters of the heart is the best medicine for mind and soul because attending to fresh wounds is easier than healing festering ones.

Village children will be encouraged to take part in their local governing councils. From the earliest possible age, inspired children can practice the skills of discourse by learning how to present an idea while also learning how to respond to counter-ideas. By participating in their local government from an early age, children will grow up to be skilled debaters, creative problem solvers and consummate team players.

As youngsters begin apprenticeships, their experience in home government will have prepared them to participate gainfully in company management. When children participate in their neighborhood and company councils from an early age, each of them will have ample opportunity to develop their leadership skills; so in future generations, the most able (rather than the most privileged) people will take the lead roles in business and government.

You would probably be happier living in a village. You would certainly get more for your money. With so many forces drawing people apart, living with others close by is the best way to create a loving home to share with good people. When considering investing in a share of a village, you might be able to do an old-fashioned cost-benefit analysis between where you're living now and how you could be living in a private-commonwealth estate.

Eight

People's Corporation

1.–New Crossroads

A ncient travelers coming upon important crossroads encountered people from near and far trading with one another in impromptu marketplaces. Caravans pitched camp nearby the open-air bazaar. Wayfarers of every sort mingled on the common grounds. As they fussed and haggled over the merchandise, fellow travelers were entertained by tall tales told by strange people from faraway lands. A few curious travelers longed for the opposite horizon and the unknown territory beyond it while many yearned to finish their business and return home. Other more enterprising individuals recognized an opportunity to become professional traders. The first merchants made their living not by growing, hunting or making stuff, instead they stayed put and traded in whatever commodities, materials and finished goods came their way. Enterprising merchants re-settled near the crossroads and established enduring marketplaces.

As regional trade expanded, grand bazaars became prominent districts of growing cities. In ancient marketplaces, strangers spoke different tongues, so sign language was a vital tool of ancient commerce. The first bookkeepers recorded transactions by impressing marks on clay tablets (with a set of specially carved sticks) to symbolically represent the items and quantities. The widespread use of clay tablets spurred the further development of writing, branding, accounting and contract law. The growing sophistication of commerce inspired the refinement of both spoken and written language.

Many modern businesses got their start in ancient cauldrons of free enterprise. No doubt marketplaces catered to voyagers. Traveling parties, probably weary of hunting, likely eyed a merchant in the marketplace cooking a pot of tasty grub and offered a trade for a meal. The restaurant business began when enterprising cooks discovered they could earn a living by conveniently satiating the traveler's hunger. Bartering: trading one particular thing for another particular thing, was often time consuming and inconvenient. Commonly traded goods such as grains and beans (even cocoa beans) served as widespread mediums of exchange until metal coins circulated.

Hospitality offered to weary strangers was ancient custom. Benevolent hosts ensured the survival of many travelers. Yet homespun hospitality could only go so far. When enterprising families recognized the opportunity to rent a temporary shelter to travelers and their animals, roadside inns began to appear on the outskirts of many towns. Recall the Christmas story of Jesus born outside such an ancient inn in Bethlehem.

Foragers emerged from the hinterlands: some carrying backloads and others pulling cartloads of ore, wood and bone that artisans transformed into goods. Prominent trading posts were situated at the confluence of rivers. Clay is commonly abundant in flat riverbeds: Curious feet wading into the cool watercourse sink into its silky embrace. Ancient entrepreneurs started the first pottery industry by setting up shop near a source of clay. If sales were brisk, masters took on apprentices and expanded their workshop.

Since the beginning of civilization, the country feeds the city, and farmers' markets were the first food markets. Herders sold their beasts in the marketplace and the first slaughterhouses, butcheries and tanneries set up shop. Marketplaces grew as commerce expanded. Once shoppers could afford more than the basics, they sought luxuries. Affluent consumers went past "I need" to "I want." Once artisans discovered that discriminating clientele were willing to pay more for prettier merchandise, commerce inspired artistic expression.

New technologies spurred new demands. Copper technology created a demand for copper and coppersmiths. Add a little tin to that copper and—Voilà—you have a metal harder than either—bronze. Once people discovered how to forge bronze, they couldn't live without it. Bronze cuts well and kills better. Unless there was both a copper and a tin source close by (not likely), most ancient people depended on far-reaching trade across land and sea for these now vital materials.

If something was worth transporting across long distances, it was certainly worth stealing. Bandits and pirates waylaid valuable cargo from the beginning of trade. Raiders became settlers, and the search for riches led men around the world. Expanding empires sponsored the highly risky exploration of faraway lands in search of exploitable resources. New territories in those distant lands later become many of the nations of the world today. World trade consolidated colonial empires. In this ever-more interconnected world, modern marketplaces inspired by ancient bazaars can be new crossroads.

2.–The People's Corporation

Most businesses get started by channeling money from investors to producers by way of financial intermediaries (stock markets, bond markets, venture-capital funds, investment banks, private investors). Forming a corporation, private or public, is high on the proven-methods list of pathways to prosperity. For publicly traded companies, stock and bond markets provide a convenient way for outside investors to share the risks and rewards of business ownership. A people's corporation is owned by its members. Radical as it may sound in many ways, it is rather old-fashioned and fiscally conservative. There are no outside shareholders. Shares cannot be traded on any market. There can be no stock buybacks, no insider trading, no pump-and-dump scams and no hostile takeovers. Each full-fledged member owns a share in a company, an estate and their people's corporation.

A people's corporation is a privately owned worker's cooperative which rarely sells or trades its shares. It is economically distinct in how it develops both halves of its economy: firms and households. This dual-shareholder arrangement in which members own both a share in their company and a share in their estate resolves the fundamental conflicts of interest between capital and labor, owners and workers, labor and management.

A people's corporation is not an imperial empire established by conquest and consolidated through slavery. It is a people's empire that thrives by conquering problems and emancipating us from exploitation and misinformation to live in harmony. While we certainly seek to earn as much money as possible, it won't be by exploiting workers, poisoning the environment or selling shoddy goods. Ours is an empire that does not seek endless expansion, therefore contraction. Rather it is a small empire that thrives through the wise stewardship of its human and natural resources.

The fatal flaw of American business is chief executive officers are advocates for the shareholders—Workers be damned. Most large, modern corporations are built on an imperialistic / master-slave / winner-take-all model. Clever public-relations campaigns paint rosy images of exceptional corporate citizenship. Marketers design alluring logos and contrive clever slogans to invoke warm-and-fuzzy feelings. People fall for the humbug because they want it to be true, yet investigators have too often revealed rampant corporate abuse and neglect. Degenerate corporations rarely give up their evil ways unless they are forced to. Too often, it is cheaper to cheat than to change. After losing in court and paying hefty fines for shoddy practices, unscrupulous corporations clean up their act only as much as they are legally forced to.

When a homeowner hires a tradesperson to do some repairs, there's a good chance that plumber or electrician will use every trick in their book to milk the situation for every dime they can. New tenants sign up for cable TV at a "low introductory rate," yet once the introductory period is over the rates double. Pre-approved credit card offers arrive daily promising zero-interest borrowing; yet suckers who bite the bait soon discover they were lured inside a trap. Once they are late with payments, the credit-card companies raise the interest rates and fees to ridiculous levels.

Too much business in America is spoiled by underhanded practices. Consider a humble homeowner in dire need of plumbing repairs who happens to have a cousin who is a professional plumber. Every homeowner would love to have a cool cousin able to drop by to work on their house. That cousin can come by in the evening after her regular job and make the repairs for a fair price or as a favor. That's what establishing a people's corporation is all about—forming a network of *friends in the business*. It's often parroted, "It's not what you know, rather—it's who you know." Getting ahead is about getting connected. People's corporations connect fellow shareholders in every fruitful way possible.

Make a list of your basic household and business needs and there you have it: the set of industries needed to establish a highly diversified, self-sufficient local economy. People need houses to live in, food to eat, clean water, good schools for their children and so on. By joining forces and fostering high standards of service, a well-organized network of entrepreneurs can provide better for themselves. Once a veteran electrician goes commonwealth and begins training apprentices, members will soon have a full-service electrical company to serve all their needs at home and at work. Once a dental company is up and running, everyone will have a dentist. Once the commonwealth bakery is open for business, the people will eat better bread. Once the commonwealth movie theatre opens its doors, the cozy lobby will be a new hot spot for movie lovers to gather.

When travelers passing through town happen upon a blighted Main Street of boarded-up stores and abandoned buildings, most will keep on driving. If they are surprised by a vibrant downtown, they'll pull over and park to check it out. Main Street has never been an anachronism. Main Street is back by popular demand. A people's corporation can play a big part in revitalizing desolate downtowns into attractive places to visit rather than spooky places to avoid.

Many bright business-school students have their sights set on the executive suite managing a large organization. That's one game. A people's corporation is quite a different game; however, most of the same fundamentals apply. Both games pursue prosperity, but a people's corporation is more down to Earth and close at hand. A people's corporation is a comprehensive investment scheme for people striving to create what most Americans are looking for—a safe, clean, vibrant and prosperous community. Perhaps that's the next big thing—an updated version of the American Dream.

3.–The General Company

The original entrepreneur's circle of a growing people's corporation becomes the General Company—the nucleus of the growing enterprise system—the sun around which the newly forming planets revolve. A few talented people with a penchant for management remain at the helm of the General Company to oversee the growing corporation. General Company executives will have a fundamentally easier job than managers in highly competitive industries under constant pressure to boost shareholder value. Rather than being sprawled over a wide territory with many far-flung outposts, the General Company's business will be rather straightforward and close at hand. The General Company continues to host an entrepreneur's circle. Ambitious members are bound to return to their spawning grounds—especially when they are enchanted with a great idea or flummoxed by a festering frustration.

The General Company hosts the general meeting of established companies. Holding meetings on a weekly basis likely does the trick; yet if much is afoot, representatives can convene the General Company Council as often and as long as needed. The general meeting will always be open to any member actively interested in what is being discussed, so attendance may swell when pressing matters are up for debate.

Aspiring executives and curious participants will be drawn to the raucous carousing and gamesmanship of playing a first-hand role in the management of their affairs.

The General Company of a growing people's corporation in its early years will need a temporary headquarters. I'm suggesting a large cozy house on the outskirts of town. Planners should make sure getting there won't be a problem. A dedicated shuttle bus and ride-sharing network would save gas and conserve parking spots. With a full kitchen and ample dining area, inspired cooks can keep the dedicated, hard-working staff and visitors well fed at all hours. If someone starts bragging about what a great cook they are, guess where they're going to be spending time? A cozy circle of couches in the living room serves as the formal and informal central gathering place. Bedrooms are converted into offices, yet one bedroom should be reserved for napping.

While private-commonwealth companies go about their day-to-day business, General Company executives concern themselves with the big picture of their growing portfolio of companies and estates. The General Company keeps its eyes on the future, near and far. Executives regularly ask themselves, "What is the business system and the living system going to look like a year from now?—best case?—worst case?—two years?" Executives devote a portion of their time divining the best industries to develop. They keep their eyes on the business system by regularly visiting companies at work. Touring the numerous workplaces, executives keep their eyes open to what's going on in the workplace and their ears open to inspirations and observations from people at work.

The General Company should set up a dedicated phone line for the curious public to call at all reasonable hours. An inspiring phone conversation could be a make-or-break moment for a hesitant curiosity seeker. A fresh, friendly effervescent charmer eager to sweet-talk whoever's calling makes the best first impression. Let them yak if there are no incoming calls.

Welcome to the reborn entrepreneur's circle. Now that it's a distinct entity, it would be appropriate to give this special forum a distinguishing name. How about the Beehive? the Cockpit? the Hornet's Nest? the Vortex? No rush choosing a name. Time to attend to the business at hand—launching businesses. Wise venture capitalists invest in the most promising ventures and the ones that fill the most urgent community needs. As business plans take time to develop, the General Company will nurture them at every stage of development from idea to fully developed plan. At the entrepreneur's circle, the most prominent question will always be—What's the next plan to bring to the launchpad? Gas station—that's an easy piece of the puzzle—everyone will fill up at the Commonwealth Fuel Depot. Excited entrepreneurs eagerly discuss the best use of the gas station's prime retail space. The General Company continues to survey the local people to discover every possible business they miss having nearby. Fill in the blank: "This town needs a (better)_____." Let's say there are no pizzerias on the south side of town. Perhaps a profitable opportunity beckons.

A natural leader can be appointed interim president, chairman of the board, prime minister—whatever the General Company chooses to call this exalted position. Their job is to represent the organization to the public and relate the big picture to members. They will be a new type of chief-executive officer who is simultaneously a worker advocate, a business advocate and a consumer advocate.

Entrepreneurs should learn all they can about the industries they are considering and the potential market for each business in each industry. They should snoop around to divine the public mood and take field trips to map out the local market. Anyone with their hearts set on a particular industry should consider getting a job in the field for a year or two to thoroughly learn the business.

Frustrated entrepreneurs must be able to shed their tears and move on from failing enterprises without going broke. Let's say a group of gastronomical impresarios opens a restaurant and there's a line out the door from day one—that's a hit. On the other hand, maybe a small crowd shows up every night, and after a few months there are some regulars and the reviews are good, but the books don't add up and they're hoping business will pick up. Now—they're in tHe DaNgEr ZoNe. It's time to get out, take an inventory of the lessons learned from their experience and move on to the next venture. Entrepreneurs must know when it's time to "shut 'er down," "pull the plug," "abandon ship." By reducing the losses from businesses that go bust, the General Company can finance more startups.

A General Company Buyer's Club can help members save money on major purchases by using their research abilities, negotiating skills and collective buying power to get the best deals on collective purchases. When a significant number of members are in the market for a particular high-priced item, the General Company pools their money and negotiates the best price. The General Company will probably not be able to get significantly better deals on items sold at the local mega-discount chain stores. We will probably have more success bargaining lower rates for overpriced services. Consider 5,000+ people collectively negotiating cable-TV, Internet and cell-phone rates. The General Company will have a strong bargaining position when soliciting bids from local providers. We might even consider starting our own telecom company.

A General Company Labor Agency can match job seekers with companies who need workers for a day or two or more. Many employers work with employment agencies that vet prospective hires and take care of the paperwork. Job hunters show up at labor halls ready-to-work, early every weekday morning. Job seekers start lining up in the wee hours. Restless job seekers make a habit of showing up even if the odds are low and the pickings are slim. But we won't leave the crew out in the cold too long. Turn on the lights, open up the door and invite them into the living room. Hot coffee is de rigueur. Real cream would be appreciated. The General Company Labor Hall will be no ordinary dive after all. Like all labor halls, there will be a dispatcher waiting for employers to call. Unlike most labor agencies, these humble early-weekday-morning conventicles will be encouraged to conspire amongst themselves to rustle up work. Broke people with bills to pay are naturally resourceful, and all but the faintest of heart will be willing to do anything reasonable for some cash. The General Company Labor Agency will survey workers for any insights into the local market, to be passed on to the Entrepreneur's Circle.

4.–Banking

In 1202, Leonardo de Pisa, better known as Fibonacci, published his *Liber Abaci*, or *Book of Calculations*, importing Hindu-Arabic numerals across the Mediterranean Sea from Muslim Africa to Christian Europe. This rather short and simple book also elucidated how to use the novel number system to calculate interest rates on loans and exchange rates for currencies. The Jewish money lenders of the Ghetto Nuovo in Venice were the first to adopt the new numbering system and accounting methods. On the other side of Italy, banking emerged from dark alleyways into the light of day when the Medici Family of Florence started the first modern bank more than 600 years ago. In 1494, Luca Pacioli, a Franciscan monk from Milan, published his *Summa de Arithmetica*, introducing double-entry bookkeeping to Europe.

In the early 1600s, the Dutch pioneered the joint-stock, limited-liability company, and the first stock in the Dutch East India Company went on sale. As more stocks were issued, the first stock markets began trading a little more than 400 years ago. The Bank of England, established in 1694, revolutionized national banking by issuing bonds: a way for governments to borrow from their citizens. Beginning in the early 1800s, from his headquarters in London, Nathan Rothschild led a trading network of five brothers with satellite offices in Frankfurt, Vienna, Paris and Naples. They pioneered international bond trading, currency exchange and large-scale banking to become the richest family in history. On the other side of the Atlantic Ocean in New York City, John Pierpont Morgan, the most powerful Gilded-Age banking mogul, bailed out a stock market panic in the 1890s. The preeminence of J.P.'s private economic power inspired the establishment of the Federal Reserve in 1912.

A well-managed central bank and a well-regulated commercial banking system are essential to a vibrant economy. Commercial banks turbocharge local economies with a little magic trick called the money multiplier. Banks lend money, borrowers go out and spend that money, most of which is redeposited, then loaned out and redeposited again—it's as if the same money is in several places at once. The more reliably loans are repaid, the higher the money multiplier. The higher the money multiplier, the greater the capital at work, so local economic growth is maximized.

Deviant lending institutions take advantage of struggling people's weakness for easy cash. High-interest loans on easy terms are often referred to as "predatory lending," as if citizens lived in a financial jungle. Private-commonwealth banks will neither exploit borrowers nor finance exploitation. Private-commonwealth banks will manage the accounts of non-exploitative, clean industries set to grow far into the future. The people's corporation bank will do its best to help members minimize banking expenses and help savers to achieve their savings goals.

Private-commonwealth banks will make banking boring again. Good banking is about managing the community's money to nurture the greatest possible growth—Nothing very atomic about that. People's-corporation bankers will not enjoy glitzy penthouse offices, rooftop heliports or private jets: Sorry–! Banking has a long and colorful history; and within a people's corporation, it will have a long—but not-very-colorful—future. Likewise, private commonwealth banking will not be a shabby affair. Bankers will have comfortable offices. Exceptional bankers will be celebrated for anticipating the markets and optimizing economic growth in challenging times.

5.–Insurance

Before modern insurance, members of the village or tribe took care of sick or injured kinsfolk. If someone broke a leg, the clan, the village or the guild would take care of the misfortunate, much like families care for their sick without handing anyone a bill for their services. If someone's hut burned down, the whole village would pool their resources to help the unfortunate victims rebuild.

Nowadays, people depend on insurance when misfortune strikes. It sucks to be diagnosed with a disease. It's no fun to be injured. It's a real bummer when your house burns down. To have to pay for it all on top of that can be devastating. Instead of adding insult to injury—like an injury leading to financial doom—insurance rescues hapless victims from the pit of destitution. When insurance works, people are brought back to health, things are restored, no one goes bankrupt and life goes on.

Large-scale, for-profit insurance companies charge as

much as possible for premiums and pay out as little as possible in settlements. The sales staff sweet-talks clients into paying for expensive policies, and then the legal staff does their best to deny paying out claims. If someone owns a home, a car and a business, they need car insurance, home insurance and several types of business insurance. Purchasing all that insurance may be the prudent thing to do at the beginning of the fiscal year, but at the end of the year, if policyholders have not collected on a claim, they have nothing to show for all the money they spent on insurance. Poof—as if by magic—their hard-earned money is in someone else's pocket. Conversely, the money paid to commonwealth insurance funds will not end up in anyone else's pocket. Any surplus earnings will be refunded or re-invested in the community.

In-house, not-for-profit insurance companies have none of the conflicting interests or salacious incentives that make insurance more complicated and expensive than it has to be. A well-managed, non-profit, internal insurance company could provide coverage at significantly reduced costs because they won't have a sales staff, a billing department or marketing expenses, just accountants, actuaries, adjusters and administrators. Modest premiums from each person, company and estate will flow into the silver chalice of the insurance fund to provide coverage.

Private-commonwealth insurance companies will be guardians of the people's health and safety. They will make a concerted effort to prevent injury and ill health through regular inspections, rigorous investigations and a thorough analysis of the effectiveness of every safety measure and health precaution.

6.–Healthcare

The basic infrastructure of a healthcare system serving 10,000 people would consist of a small hospital, a primary-care clinic and several peripheral clinics. The Primary Care Clinic would house enough physicians so every member has a doctor. The General Hospital would have twenty to thirty beds, be equipped to handle emergencies, house a small staff of specialists, some fancy diagnostic equipment and a few labs.

There is no workable, one-size-fits-all model when it comes to designing a local healthcare system. The first factor to consider is the capacity of the healthcare infrastructure serving the region. If there is a shortage of capacity, the people's corporation should consider building a large enough hospital to make up for the shortfall. If there is a surplus of hospital capacity, they should set their sights on a more modest hospital.

We do not wish to prevent our community from seeking healthcare, but we should discourage people from visiting the doctor for every little complaint. Each estate will minister its own first-aid and homecare. Creating a safe and healthy place to live and encouraging a healthy lifestyle will reduce the demand for healthcare by younger people, yet will increase the demand by older people as they live longer. If a hospital sets up an emergency room, they are required by law to handle any emergencies that show up at their door. A healthcare system integrated with the surrounding region should budget for a certain amount of charitable care, especially if there is an underserved local population

A remotely-located private-commonwealth municipality would require a full-spectrum healthcare system to handle its own needs and be prepared for a sizeable emergency. A city with minimal automobile infrastructure should develop its system of pathways, normally used by bikers and joggers, wide enough to handle emergency vehicles. The pathway system should be laid out so there is unobstructed access for emergency vehicles between all points in the city and the hospital.

Specialists might prefer to set up shop outside of the hospital in a satellite clinic. A mental-health clinic could be housed in a separate facility, and they should keep their doors open 24 hours a day. Tragically, people who need attention the most, often have the most difficulty finding someone to talk to. In a Land of Light, nobody should be suffering in the shadows. The light will always be on at the *Emergency Room for the Heart* for those in dire need of a shoulder to cry on and whatever medical, psychiatric and legal referrals they need.

The healthcare system works in tandem with every peripheral health practitioner such as fitness coaches, massage therapists and nutritionists. By maintaining patient records in a central medical data bank, the effectiveness of every form of therapy, exercise routine, and diet can be measured so optimal diet, exercise and meditation-relaxation regimens can be developed for each person.

Hospitals and clinics are designed with both patients and medical staff in mind. There are several reasons to build attractive medical facilities. Doctors and nurses get paid more-or-less the same wherever they work, so building a beautiful hospital attracts and retains staff. Comfortable hospital bedrooms, alluring indoor atriums and enchanting outdoor gardens have been proven to lift the mood of patients and help their recovery.

7.–Business Nursery

Over the last fifty years, hundreds of business incubators have helped thousands of manufacturers get their enterprises off to a strong start. Industrial-support systems of many sorts have become part of the manufacturing landscape in many parts of the world. They enrich local economies by supporting innovation, creating jobs and fattening city and county tax coffers. Traditional business incubators specialize in high-tech, cutting-edge, multimillion-dollar startups. What is proposed here serves a similar purpose yet is more homespun, costs less and has a different name.

The term *business nursery* is appropriate because nurseries are places where both animals and plants are nurtured from birth. This rather humble business nursery is designed to help ambitious hobbyists and aspiring artisans develop their home-based enterprises into profitable businesses. They'll sell their goods in a retail marketplace, called here *The Bazaar* and develop their product lines with the support of, what is named here, *The Cottage Industry Development Company.*

This plan for a business nursery was inspired by the many flea markets and swap meets that were more prominent features of American commercial culture in past decades. This model is also inspired by the passionate hobbyists whose true love is what they do after work in their garage or basement. In today's high-tech, competitive marketplace, home-based entrepreneurs will have a much greater chance of success with the help of a knowledgeable, resourceful and helpful support system. The aim is for businesses to outgrow the Nursery to be transplanted to permanent locations downtown, in the Marketplace or the Industrial Park.

Let's envision the Bazaar getting started on a five-acre grass lot fronting a prominent roadway. The marketplace would begin rather humbly much like a traditional flea market with vendors parking in designated spots and displaying their wares on folding tables. As the marketplace grows, it should do its best to preserve an open-air setting with a festive, bare-foot, family atmosphere. Fun and games are encouraged: volleyball, badminton, picnic tables and game boards. When enough local growers show up, the Bazaar sets aside a promi-nent area for a farmer's market. The Cottage Industry De-velopment Company gets started in a sturdy tent or trailer. They experiment with various arrangements of temporary structures before building any permanent ones.

The Business Nursery a.k.a. Bazaar spreads word near and far to attract talented and ambitious artisans, hobbyists and tinkerers: seamstresses, leatherworkers, jewelers, woodwork-ers, potters, metal workers, shoemakers, musical-instrument makers and artisanal-food producers. When the guidance to get started and the resources to keep growing are readily available, restless tradespeople and frustrated hobbyists will be inspired to participate. They begin their entrepreneurial journey by sitting down with a counselor to get their wheels spinning. Veterans advise dreamers to bring them down to Earth and get them up to speed. Every kind of cooperation is encouraged because it will take several principals to develop a company capable of leaving the Nursery. The Business Nursery could sponsor trips to regional or national conven-tions for practitioners to keep up with the latest in their industry.

Many hobbyists are in the dark when it comes to sourcing the best suppliers. They likely don't know about resources such as the *Thomas Register,* the largest directory of industrial suppliers for more than a century, (renamed since I last used it: *Thomasnet.com*) nor do they have the inclination to spend a lot of time searching for the best sources for all they purchase for their business. The Cottage Industry Development Company does the research to discover the best suppliers for tools, materials and services in much the same way manufacturers and large retailers employ professional buyers to assure getting the best deals from wholesalers, suppliers and subcontractors.

After some time, the Cottage Industry Development Company can set up a display of tools and materials to pique the public's curiosity and encourage the development of unexplored industries. Such a showroom would be able to display only a token sampling of all the small machines in the industrial universe. The purpose of the showroom is to display machines not available in retail stores such as rivet presses, lathes, industrial sewing machines, lost-wax metal-casting equipment, shoe-making equipment. Industrial-grade machines display beauty in their practicality. Shiny tools on display to the curious public will beckon to be put to good use. If it's not on display; they can order it, and the friendly staff will use their leverage and knowhow to get you the best deal.

The Bazaar will only be as financially strong as the sales of the businesses it sponsors—the Bazaar and its vendors sink or float together. The Bazaar supports itself by collecting a percentage of sales rather than rent. Twenty percent is suggested as a working figure. With standard-issue cash registers linked to a central data bank, the Bazaar can precisely measure the sales of each company to decipher trends and recognize buying patterns.

The Cottage Industry Development Company hosts its own venture-capital company to finance promising startups, akin to micro-lending institutions pioneered in emerging countries. Borrowing even a small sum of money should never be easy, so the loan officers' job is to thoroughly vet prospective borrowers. But for good reason—if the Bazaar is to succeed, its venture-capital company must join forces with profitable businesses that pay back their loans on time.

At business meetings, everyone with skin in the game gathers. Venders will be admonished to balance their company interests with common concerns. There may be turf disputes. Every company naturally wants the best location possible, yet the Council focuses on figuring out which arrangement serves everyone best. Using sales data, they consider the best way to move the pieces around their chessboard. Perhaps fledgling companies can start in the front, and as they gain a following, move a step or two back. Many retailers are convinced corner stores do best. In big square tents divided in four, four businesses can have a corner location. Perhaps a circular arrangement is the most equitable and leaves a large open space in the middle. For concerts, picture a stage facing a basketball-court sized (or slightly larger) courtyard with food, drink and merch venders lining the open area.

After a year or two, thriving businesses bursting at the seams will be dying to move to larger facilities custom built for their enterprise. The conundrum at the core of the Business Nursery's business model is how it loses income by succeeding at its mission of facilitating the birth of profitable businesses. There are several possible ways to make up for this loss. Traditional business incubators and accelerators retain a stake in the companies they helped create. Even a half-percent stake in a company could be a small but steady income for the Nursery. Successful alumni are known to donate to their alma maters. The Bazaar could host an outlet selling wares produced by companies they nurtured. The Bazaar could retain a monopoly on the sale of ready-to-eat food. The *Bazaar Bar* might be a cash cow. Profitable enterprises that don't gain enough traction to leave the Bazaar could make it their home.

The nighttime is the right time to cater to people looking for some fun. As the sun nears the horizon, the Bazaar general marketplace closes while the food and entertainment venues surrounding the courtyard remain open. The bar will open and the band will begin to play. People who discover the Bazaar during the day will be encouraged to come back for the nighttime fun. People who discover the nighttime good times will be encouraged to check out the Bazaar during the day.

8.–Industrial Park

The consumer-goods market is the most visible and publicly promoted part of the economy. The industrial market is nearly as big, yet not very visible to those working outside of it. Consider the clothing industry and the industrial market behind the consumer market. Clothing makers depend on material suppliers and sewing-machine makers. Textile mills depend on suppliers of spinning, weaving and knitting machines and raw cotton, silk and nylon. Sewing-machine makers depend on other manufacturers and suppliers for the machines and materials they use to make their machines.

In the heyday of American manufacturing, Gilded-Age moguls controlled every part of the production process. Today, manufacturers worldwide operate in ever-more interdependent networks of suppliers and subcontractors. The more complicated the final product, the more complex the network of factories and workshops needed to produce that product. Commercial jetliners are some of the most complicated machines made today. Both Boeing and Airbus outsource parts from dozens of countries to build their marvelous flying machines.

The bygone days of factory workers toiling away on assembly lines performing a single repetitive task are long gone. Nowadays, factory work is much more brainy than brawny. Due to the efficiency of modern equipment, the newest manufacturing plants employ fewer workers with greater skills. Factory floors have transformed from lively places with hundreds of workers to lonely places with only a few dozen workers in sight.

The original mega-factories of days gone by were famous for smokestacks towering hundreds of feet above the industrial landscape. Smokestacks are icons of a bygone era, yet big production facilities are not going out of style. At the opposite end of the spectrum, many small-scale manufacturers make their homes in industrial parks: clusters of small factories sharing common resources usually located in suburban areas and outer districts served by highways, railroads and canals.

People's corporation industrial parks are developed with facilities for up to one hundred small factories. There you will find the noisy, dirty, potentially dangerous machinery not appropriate for a retail marketplace. Successful industrial parks widen the diversity of the local economy and create jobs. Prudent city commissioners will go out of their way to attract low-impact industries to boost their local economy.

Industrial property on a waterway is ideal to host maritime industries that fabricate and service boats and barges. Industrial parks served by railroad lines can develop heavier industries made possible by the super-heavy loads only railroads can haul over land. In any case, industrial-park developers consider which industries would benefit the most from the modes of transportation available.

Industrial-park factories are more heavy-duty and high-tech than retail-marketplace workshops. They are also much more expensive to equip than craft workshops. Industrial sewing machines sell for around $1,000. A woodworking shop can purchase a high-quality table saw for about $3,000. Computer-operated machine tools sell for tens of thousands of dollars and higher. High-tech printing presses can cost into the millions. The machines to equip a small industrial company could easily cost several hundred thousand dollars to begin with and millions of dollars over the long run.

Small factories in remote locations are at a disadvantage in several respects. With only ten principal workers, a private-commonwealth-industrial company's economies of scale are limited. Transportation in and out of remote locations takes longer and costs more. Fortunately, each new generation of machines is more efficient, and companies could transcend many of the limitations of their limited size by joining forces with other Industrial Park and Marketplace companies.

Consider an industrial park dedicated to motor vehicles established on a properly zoned ten-acre property at the edge of town. Everywhere you go (by car) there is a steady demand for automotive services. Many car owners are still looking for a mechanic they can trust. Automotive industrialists can get started on a shoestring doing simple repairs and oil changes. From humble beginnings, there is great potential for growth by diversification without enormous capital outlays. There is a broad spectrum of automotive specialty shops possible—body, paint, transmission, tire, restoration, conversion, air conditioning and engine rebuilding to start the list. Aside from cars, vans, pickup trucks and motorcycles; there are bigger commercial vehicles and a wide range of smaller vehicles—scooters, snowmobiles, golf carts, all-terrain, pint-size construction vehicles and lawn equipment. A fully developed motor-vehicle conglomerate would be able to establish a true one-stop auto marketplace for buying, selling, repairs, custom-rebuilds and salvage.

9.–Construction Company Conglomerate

When I was growing up in New York City, I gazed down upon many impressive excavations through small openings in the plywood perimeter fences. After the hole was dug, enormous concrete foundations were poured five stories below street level. Over the coming months, monster steel skeletons climbed skyward from those foundations. Little did I know I would spend many years working in the construction trades and go from building houses to proposing grand plans for building an entire city.

Optimistic futurism evokes visions of fantastic cityscapes of shimmering silver spires interspersed with flying automobiles zooming down multilevel skyways. Such fantastic visions can only be actualized in a harmonious future. Humankind must figure out what to do about the billion malnourished people on the planet before they start flying their swank jet-mobiles to party on the 300th floor of opulent sky-towers.

The New World must be built from the ground up. Trailblazers get started by climbing ladders, sweating in their tool belts and banging a few nails. The following rudimentary business plan is based on my experience as a professional carpenter and residential remodeler. If construction is not your thing, with a little imagination you can apply many parts of this template to the industry you are dreaming of.

A private-commonwealth construction conglomerate grows by diversifying into the numerous construction fields: electrical, plumbing, painting, roofing, siding, landscaping. Each company carefully earns their reputation in the community one job at a time. The construction conglomerate builds its reputation in the local and regional market one project at a time.

The construction industry runs the gamut from neighborhood repairmen to large-scale commercial construction companies. There is a wide spectrum of professionals and tradespeople in the construction industry from nerdy architects wearing skinny ties working in air-conditioned offices to brawny road warriors wielding ninety-pound jack hammers working in the hot sun dripping with sweat. There are a lot of ex-military in the construction field because a martial style of organization can work well in construction. Teams of workers are deployed into the field with their tools to get a mission done and return back safe. There is an art to building. The foreman choreographs the grand production making sure everyone moves across the stage without bumping into each other.

During the many phases of a building project, the different trades work side by side. One trade's good work depends on the trades that came before them. Let's say the carpenters frame some sloppy walls. The drywall crew can do little to improve warped walls. The painters, no matter how skillfully they apply their paint, cannot straighten crooked walls. Managing a building project involves complex logistics: having the right people, materials and tools where and when they are needed in the many steps of a long process. Productivity at the jobsite is based on preparation, organization and teamwork.

Running an efficient organization is key to prospering in any industry. Good communication increases both productivity and efficiency. The more thoroughly the crew discusses the job before, during and after the workday, the smoother it will go. I've had great conversations with my bosses on the way to and from work; and believe me, I picked their brains for every morsel of knowledge I could glean. I've spent many hours talking to fellow carpenters and tradespeople in coffee shops, bars and other informal gatherings. It's only natural for people to talk about what they do all day long. I'm just advising budding construction companies to take full advantage of tradespeople's natural desire to babble about their trade.

A growing amalgamation of construction companies should find a home in which to grow: part workshop, part clubhouse, part garage. With a home base; if it's a cold, ugly day; the crew can cancel work in the field and catch up with work in the shop. In a fully equipped shop, there are more tools at the crew's disposal than could ever be conveniently lugged into the field. In a shop, both solo endeavors and group projects can come to life. Workers spend their daylight hours at the jobsite or in the shop cranking out proven money-makers; while after hours, insomniacs burn the midnight oil tinkering with special projects and tweaking masterpieces.

Many components used in residential and commercial buildings can be custom built in a workshop: cabinets, countertops, doors, windows, cupolas. Woodworking is often held in low esteem—Like you want to spend your working life building bird houses, yet I beg to differ—The finest violins sell for $30,000, and the finest pianos sell for prices on par with high-end sports cars: $250,000 or thereabouts. A large enough shop can be used to build stage and movie sets. The credits at the end of most movies list carpenters. Harrison Ford got his big break going from fiddle farting as a carpenter on movie sets to rescuing the galaxy in *Star Wars*—I'm jealous.

Nine

Estate Development

1.–Declare Your Real Estate Independence

T he best way to contain real estate and housing costs in any market or economy is to buy together and build together. The greatest hurdle a people's corporation must overcome to claim independence in the real estate wilderness is raising the rather substantial sum of money needed to develop their first estate. A home for one hundred people is a multimillion-dollar project, and it is impractical for estate founders to vacate their houses and apartments before their deluxe new home is ready.

A people's corporation might be able to finance only one estate at a time to start, yet after christening their first estate, it should get easier with experience. Second-generation estates will model themselves on first-generation estates, third-generation estates will draw inspiration from both, and so the system will grow. Estates can host businesses, yet an estate might choose not to host a business because residents prefer not to. On the other hand, if a money-making opportunity beckons, it is wise to take advantage of it. After all, estate developers almost certainly paid for the privilege. In downtown locations, street-level retail is the way to go. Suburban estates bordering busy roads may have properties ideal for roadside retail or hospitality. Choice rural properties may be suitable to develop into enchanting resorts.

Estates hosting businesses enjoy a double advantage. When business is slow, idle workers can retreat to their cozy homes. If business picks up unexpectedly, extra help will be close at hand. Estate residents can ever-so conveniently patronize their establishments: eating in (or ordering out from) their restaurants, riding their horses or having a good ol' time at their roadside club.

The better an estate is designed today, the more its residents will enjoy it in the days to come. A home for one hundred people requires seventy to eighty bedrooms organized in studio, one-, two- and three-bedroom apartments in one or several buildings. Estate developers should scout out suitable properties to start a list for comparison. Once planners have actual properties under consideration, budding designers will be inspired to break out their sketch pads. Promising plans can be detailed on computer-aided-design programs so everyone interested in the project can share their observations and concerns. Hobbyists can build scale models. Accountants can make cost comparisons. Developers can use their models and drawings to entice potential residents to consider taking a share in their future village.

Organized sporting leagues inspire dedication, camaraderie and competition. Estates with baseball fields form a baseball league. Estates with tennis courts join forces to form an estate tennis league. With fields and courts close by, *estaters* will be inspired to get off their couches and head for the baseball field to hit that grand slam or make their way to the tennis courts to vanquish every challenger—at the very least, have some fun and get some exercise.

In private-commonwealth estates, all sorts of informal learning will be happening in community kitchens, workshops and playing fields. However, when it comes to formal education, nothing beats state-of-the-art classrooms, workshops and studios. Once the regular school day is over, an estate can commandeer their school for extracurricular academic, vocational and recreational classes. Education entrepreneurs start by surveying the townsfolk to determine what the local people are eager to learn to advance their careers, indulge their curiosities or advance their hobby skills. After surveying who is available to teach (what and when), educators can schedule a wide range of classes.

A people's corporation with a growing network of companies and estates scattered all over town and out into the country should run a transportation system. I recommend letting anarchy reign before imposing order. To get things going, bands of local, freelance, passenger-van drivers who grew up in the neighborhood and have lots of friends can experiment with routes and times. After some experience, drivers will have a logbook of how many hours they worked, how many miles they drove, how much they spent on gas and after counting their take precisely how much money they made on each run and for each day.

Drivers solicit suggestions from talkative passengers. By keeping records of the demand for transportation along various routes, drivers will soon have a good idea of what will work best. The fledgling transportation company then uses their observations and data to plot the most efficient routes and determine how early, how late and how often it is worth covering each route. A transportation company could double as a school-bus system. A transportation fleet could triple as a parcel service that delivers custom orders from the Marketplace or prescriptions from the Pharmacy. The transportation company could join forces with (by sharing drivers and vehicles) with a taxi company or long-distance coach bus service.

2.–Urban Estates

Urban-estate developers have two ways to go. They can build apartment buildings from the ground up or remodel suitable commercial properties. Occupied apartment buildings have long-time residents with long-term leases and long-standing ties to the community. Purchasing an occupied apartment building to convert into an estate, developers would have to give residents the boot when their leases run out, and they won't make any friends or gain any respect doing that. Defunct hotels are probably more suitable to remodel into urban estates because they have none of the resident problems, and their general layout is likely more suitable for an urban estate. Apartments can be single, double or triple room. Grand lobbies, banquet halls, restaurants, ball rooms, V.I.P. suites and penthouses can be converted into the common grounds of elegant vertical villages.

In big cities, the stakes are higher and the risks are greater. The least expensive urban properties are found in neighborhoods that have fallen on hard times. Urban blight can present a golden opportunity for estate developers. Since people have fled once prospering and beloved neighborhoods, decay dominates the landscape. Many cities offer subsidized loans and grants to encourage urban development in blighted areas. Big city or small, the same basic set of design principles apply for developing apartment-building estates.

Ever since manufacturers began relocating away from city centers, decommissioned factories have been converted into attractive residential spaces in downtown warehouse districts. The interior spaces are called lofts because their ceilings are high enough for a sleeping loft or even a mezzanine. Factory buildings are solidly built to support heavy machinery. High ceilings are matched by tall windows. Many loft buildings have loading docks and extra-large service elevators that make moving in and out a breeze. The top floor likely has skylights to flood the community space with sunlight. Flat rooftops can be developed into recreation areas. Many warehouse districts are the trendiest part of town making them ideal for street-level and second-floor retail.

Decommissioned schools commonly have a sizeable number of classrooms in the main building, alongside a wing with a gymnasium and a theater. A combination of buildings and ball fields could be ideal for an urban-estate campus. If there is a cement play yard, it should be demolished and replaced by a grassy field. Spacious administrative offices flanking dilapidated lobbies could be converted into a swank lobby and a trendy café. Developers should do all they can to make good use of the theater, getting started by showing movies with the remaining old-school equipment. Drama would be a little more involved: an estate would have to attract a theatre or dance troop to set up shop. Estate planners creatively remodel their gymnasium and playing fields so residents are inspired to stay fit.

Break it down—The word *apartment* begins with the word *apart*—yet apartment buildings can be tranquil refuges. Rather than riding a lonely elevator and opening the door to an empty apartment, you will come home to a lively urban village. After walking through the grand front entrance, you're greeted by your concierge—Any messages? You can check out the schedule of the evening's activities, or just lounge in the lobby to see who shows up. To your left—a movie poster of what's playing in the theater tonight. Maybe you're in the mood to take a dip in the rooftop swimming pool. Perhaps you're in a studious mood and the fourth-floor library is calling. Maybe you just can't make up your mind, so you head to your swank abode to wind down. You can always come out to play later on tonight.

3.–Suburban Estates

Suburban-estate developers will have a chill assignment searching for properties. In the mood for some local road tripping? As you're heading out of town, the land opens up with fields and forests. The farther from town you venture, the bigger the lots and the lower the prices. Searchers keep their eyes out for pristine parcels of five to twenty acres.

In a two- or three-story courtyard apartment building,

every apartment would be *apart from* and *a part of* the village. Every apartment's front door would face the courtyard—the magic sunlit, moonlit, starlit open space. Residents can enjoy the comforts of home; and whenever they're in the mood for company, there'll probably be people having fun right outside their front door. Picture residents chillin' on their balcony, reading a neighbor's novel while watching the children at play in the lively courtyard below. The community kitchen rings the dinner bell—Supper's ready. There's a performance after dinner at the far end of the courtyard. From balconies on three sides, spectators can watch the show seated just a few feet from the comforts of home.

I was architecturally inspired by a visit to Chaco Culture National Historical Park in New Mexico. Chaco Canyon features the restored ruins of an ancient Anasazi city that thrived for three centuries from about A.D. 850. Below the northern rim of the canyon are the ruins of a very large 1,000-year-old building Spanish explorers named *Pueblo Bonito*. Anthropologists estimate about 600 people lived and worshipped in that building at the height of their civilization. Pueblo Bonito is shaped like a horseshoe with the open-end facing south, so direct sunlight shines on every wall, window and doorway facing the inside of the horseshoe. In a two-or-three story, crescent-shaped open-courtyard apartment building, every apartment would overlook the courtyard and the southern horizon. Every apartment would enjoy direct sunlight for most of the day. Flower gardens and cascading waterways would create a lush garden environment.

Suburban estates with frontage on a prominent road should consider developing roadside businesses. Picture a honky-tonk (juke joint if you prefer) and motel on a not-so-lonely highway on the outskirts of town. A successful club and motel would create a healthy supply of jobs. Estaters will be fighting for the best bartending shifts. Community stages should have a backstage door for performers and a loading dock for their equipment—dressing rooms if feasible. To cater to a broad spectrum of tastes, the club alternates its musical flavor each weeknight: Metal Mondays, Country Tuesdays, Hip-hop Wednesdays, Jazz Thursdays. Open-mic nights will give novices an opportunity to see if they have what it takes to evoke laughter or inspire applause.

4.–Rural Estates

Many sophisticated city dwellers hold slanted concepts of country folks as simple-minded, gun-toting, fundamentalist nut-jobs. City-slickers are the real nature lovers. They cherish a hike through the woods hoping to catch a glimpse of some wildlife to shoot a few photographs to preserve their precious memories. Country people do the other kind of shooting. Yet wily characterizations of county people are exaggerations fueled by stereotypes propagated by the dramatic proclivities of Hollywood producers. Most country folk are mighty fine, level-headed people city folk would be delighted to meet. Are you ready to explore the country?

Country living has a lot going for it—cheaper land, less crime, beautiful night skies, cleaner air, agricultural opportunities on farmland, recreational opportunities in woods, meadows and lakes. Rural-estate developers will be on the lookout for properties they can transform into tranquil and dynamic havens. Their goal is to take a raw parcel of land and develop it into a place people want to live and visit.

The facilities a rural estate can develop depend on the land they have to work with. At the edge of a National Forest, an estate will have a wilderness nearby. Open meadows surrounded by forests makes good horse country. Lakeside living can be quite enchanting: swimming, diving, fishing and boating. A small private lake might be ideal, while frontage on a large lake (ringed with other resorts) would be more exciting, but noisier and busier.

Rural-estate developers take epic weekend camping trips to explore territories. Picture a rustic wooded property surrounding a secluded lake. After walking the land and swimming in the lake, worn-out day-trippers magically transform into campfire visionaries glowing in the firelight brainstorming grand plans. Rural estates develop their recreational facilities and purchase their equipment for their member's enjoyment, keeping future guests in mind of course. Lakeside residents will get plenty of enjoyment out of their canoes before visitors show up to join the fun.

When developing a woodland property, we will preserve the forest canopy by conserving the healthiest, widest and tallest trees. To prevent the spread of fire, standing-dead trees are felled, tree stumps are pulled out, low-hanging dead branches are removed, and the forest floor is cleared of any gnarly underbrush—all good ways to prevent forest fires—all good bonfire material—all making for a civilized and accessible forest.

Rural estates can generate electricity from solar panels, wind turbines and, with a stream flowing down a steep-enough hill, mini-hydroelectric power plants. A propane or diesel-fueled power plant would probably generate the most juice in the smallest amount of space and propane or diesel can be trucked in. To conserve energy costs, the power plant for a twenty- to thirty-bedroom lodge would shut down each evening after most people are asleep and energy demands are the lowest. The other buildings on the property would each have their own power system. With a decentralized system with parallel backup systems, residents will rarely run out of electricity. When a system runs out of juice, the lights won't be as bright and there'll be stuff they won't be able to do until that particular power system comes back online.

5.–Rural Rehab

Rural estates can host rehabilitation centers. Such estates would enjoy the advantages of low overhead costs and remote, tranquil and spacious settings. This particular essay is about a rural rehab dedicated to helping people stop smoking cigarettes and inhaling vaping products. Tobacco-cessation retreats would be fully voluntary. Tobacco is not illegal, so nicotine addicts would not be court-ordered to attend. Tobacco products are not risky to quit like hard drugs or alcohol, so there would be no need for a doctor on call. Cigarette smokers spend a lot of money to keep up with their habit and in addition pay a big price in reduced vitality, lost productivity and extra medical expenses. Many long-time smokers would be willing to invest some of their hard-earned savings to end their dependence on nicotine. I'm sure most of them wouldn't mind getting out of town for a while.

Tens of millions of people have successfully quit smoking tobacco, so how difficult can it really be? It's not like climbing Mt. Everest. Tobacco addiction is a round-the-clock craving that comes back begging for satisfaction every half hour or so. People quit tobacco by flipping a mental switch to *off* and discovering the fortitude to never let it flip back *on*. Before they know it, people who successfully quit are feeling better, saving money and wondering why they ever started smoking in the first place.

The magic bus has arrived at its remote destination. Tobacco-craving city-slickers behold their idyllic, timeless, temporary home hidden deep in the majestic forest. After settling in; come evening, the small rural community gathers to discuss their addiction to the wicked weed. Professional counselors guide the assembled lunatics to sanity. Aspiring quitters pour their hearts out praying all the pain will inspire them to quit once and for all time. They knock themselves up the side of the head screaming "Why can't I just quit? Why can't I just stop once and for all time? What the Hell is wrong with me?" Such public displays of painful yearning are good for the soul in any case. Call it constructive suffering if you like. Over the coming days or weeks, visitors are availed to a variety of activities to keep them busy physically, mentally and socially.

In a comfortable yet totally tobacco-free environment, captives will not need to exercise self-discipline when the substance they crave is simply not available. Isolated in a comfortable country retreat, nicotine addicts can relax because the inner battle is won for the duration of their stay. The whole want-to–don't-want-to, should–shouldn't inner-conflict soon becomes futile. The whole war raging in the tobacco addict's mind fades away after a few days when there is no tobacco to be had. Cravers will think they are going crazy but pretty soon they'll realize they are actually becoming sane. They will fidget and fuss yet before long they will calm down. Guests are given lessons in healthy living and coping with stress. Before they know it, they loosen up, start to have fun and begin to reconnect with the natural wonder of life they probably haven't felt for a while. Yet staff must keep an eye on visitors so they are not tempted to go astray.

Armed guards posted at the gates will shoot smokers on sight, so captives dare not cheat. Resistance will be futile. A crocodile-infested moat and electrified barbed-wire fences surrounding the compound will make escape impossible. All kidding aside, once cravings diminish, visitors return home refreshed and many will never light up or vape again.

6.–Mountain Monastery

Modern people are attracted to monastic living for the same reasons as the original malcontents drawn to the first Buddhist monasteries two-and-a-half thousand years ago. For certain people, pursuing a career and clamoring for social prestige doesn't seem worth the effort or the rewards. Conventional living is a disappointment and worldly pursuits have little savor. The world feels hollow and shallow so searchers long for something solid and deep. Hardcore devotees will make the monastery their home. They will discover contented lives up in the hills, far removed from the ball of confusion they left behind. Some enthusiasts will stay for long stretches of time: Forty days, usually in silence (don't bet on it), is a tradition in imitation of Jesus' forty days in the desert. Secluded bastions encouraging clean living can also be great places to get some serious study and research done.

Do you ever get the urge to drive deep into the woods with a bunch of friends to a special spot to have a big weekend party under the stars and country sunshine? Be my guest. Just promise to clean up when you're done. And remember, partying gets old after a while. Private-commonwealth-estate monasteries will be the ultimate place to escape the party scene. While most rural estates develop facilities to pursue a wide range of recreational activities to indulge in every kind of exercise or sporting activity, private-commonwealth monasteries will be remote places established for the pursuit of more austere forms of recreation.

Most of us wish we could save more and squander less, and that is just what early monastics did. If each of us could recoup the money we have squandered over the years, most of us would reap quite a bonanza. It doesn't cost that much money to just live, but it does cost a decent amount of money to live well. After all, money is meant to be spent. Paradoxically, many monastic orders took vows of poverty, then grew wealthy from their thrift and industry. Monastic living does not focus on the next fancy thing you want to buy, rather on all the fancy things you can get by without.

Inspired by the writings of Thomas Merton, monasteries recaptured the popular imagination beginning in the 1950s. Martial-arts films glamorized remote mountain dojos, very similar to religious monasteries, where kung-fu practitioners perfected their skills. Yet in both Asia and Europe, monasteries are well past their heyday. Of the several thousand monasteries that once thrived, several hundred have survived to function in our modern day. In addition, hundreds of long-abandoned monasteries lie in magnificent ruins awaiting pilgrims and international tourists. Over the last few decades, a New Monasticism Movement has spawned the development of a fresh generation of nontraditional monasteries.

Some historians claim the Industrial Revolution of the nineteenth century was inspired by the monasteries of the Middle Ages. Medieval monks and nuns followed a regular schedule, carefully marshaled their resources and didn't squander their surpluses. Monastics saved more, wasted less and forsook frivolities. Their way of living encouraged the development of highly refined agriculture and food craft; hence the highest-quality cheeses, wines and beers. Dom Pérignon, namesake of the world's most famous champagne, was a Benedictine monk. Whiskey was perfected by Irish monks. Nowadays, foods and beverages produced in monasteries carry a cachet of craftsmanship and purity and sell at top-shelf prices.

The monastery is an ancient concept, long in the making, ripe for rebirth in the turbulent twenty-first century. Picture a majestic mountain monastery deep in the misty mountains. Welcome to the forest primeval. There is no disturbing evening news once you are truly off-the-grid and out-of-signal-range. Getting back to the simple life has never been out of style. Everyone should try it sometime. Getting away from the hustle and bustle of the world grants perspective. Life is very short, they say—yet truly—Life is very long indeed, and what a blessing to have it all reflected into one moment of clarity. Breathe deep the crisp mountain air. Stop letting your imagination run wild. Now is the best opportunity you'll ever have to release all that tension and indulge in some deep relaxation. Things are probably not as bad as you think. Behold the magnificent countryside visible in every direction. Maybe you've gotten your priorities mixed up and lost sight of what really matters.

As long as you're willing to chop wood, carry water and help with a few chores, you can stay. Clean living has a way of growing on you. We could really use someone like you around here. You might come to prefer the cloistered life. The basic advantage of a tranquil lifestyle is you never rush to get anything done, yet still get an amazing amount accomplished.

The cottage industries that can be developed to lend support to a monastery will depend on the natural resources at hand. Rough mountainous terrain is ideal for goats, and goats can be a lot of fun. Rolling meadows are good sheep country. If there are flowery meadows nearby, beekeeping is definitely something to consider.

Real monasteries will take real money to materialize. Rugged mountain roads are rough on vehicles. To build a remote stronghold in the mountains, monastics would have to do much more than sell their goat cheese, wool sweaters and jars of honey in town. Calculating a modern monastery's value may prove challenging. Developers must consider how much money the 10,000 shareholders of a people's corporation are willing to invest for the "priceless" resource of a remote mountain sanctuary within driving distance of home. Those who become enamored with the idea should search for some generous seed-money donors. Maybe a pair of people's corporations could pursue a joint venture midway between their domains. Whatever the situation, monasteries will generate modest incomes, certainly never enough to cover all the expenses needed to maintain them.

Since their beginning, monastic orders depended on the donations of wealthy patrons. Medieval monks were expected to forsake their worldly possessions and claims to property. Candidates from wealthy families bequeathed substantial gifts to gain entry into their order. Long-established Catholic monastic orders: Dominican, Franciscan, Jesuit,

Cistercian and Trinitarian are famous for the rule books defining their way of life. Modern monastic pioneers will have to get quite contemplative when devising the rules for their new order. They must clearly define their mission and clarify their purpose:

First—What precisely are residents and visitors hoping to accomplish?

Next—What exactly are the values the monastery stands for?

Finally—What restrictions must be put in place to accomplish their purposes? Should visitors leave their laptops at home? If there's good game in the woods, can residents go hunting? Is the main building going to be built with vaulted ceilings and stained-glass windows or do developers have a more oriental architectural flavor in mind? I'm trying to be amusing, but some serious soul searching and brainstorming will be needed to forge a sustainable monastic vision for the twenty-first century.

7.–Bringing Back the Family Farm

Americans forever chase the novel. As the United States industrialized, country living came to symbolize an idyllic past while modern cities beckoned the future. Cities are sexy. Why toil your whole life away working in the dirt when you can live a good, clean life in a modern city? But the novelty has worn off. Cities have grown expensive, overcrowded and dirty, so now moving back to the farm is the novel thing to do.

In the mid-1830s, Henry Blair, the second African American ever awarded a patent, introduced his mechanical corn-and-cotton planting machines. In 1840, Cyrus McCormick sold his first mechanical harvesters. In 1892, John Froelich introduced the first gasoline-powered farm tractor and over the coming decades farmers transitioned form horsepower to tractor power. As labor-saving technology advanced, displaced farmers have continually migrated to urban centers. Traditional family farms have been consolidated into modern "factory farms" growing vast fields of a single crop. The industrialization of farming has alienated most people from civilization's rich agricultural heritage. From America's earliest colonial settlements to the present, the portion of people living on farms has gone from seventy percent to two percent: from a vast majority to a tiny minority of the people.

The very survival of humankind depends on farms. Wall Street stock brokers and hedge-fund managers relish their power at the center of the financial universe—yet truly—farms are the foundation of the economy. The farm and the village are a classic combination going back through the millennia to the very beginning of agriculture and animal husbandry. Farm estates will value more than crop yields and commodity prices. Farm-estate residents will enjoy the deep satisfaction and security of growing their own food.

Agriculture inspired some of the first science. Innovative farmers cross-pollinated their hardiest plants to breed ever-stronger varieties of the grains, fruits and vegetables they grew. The first oxen conveniently pooped in the field ahead of the plow they were pulling, so the first farmers quickly learned the value of fertilizing the soil with manure. People grew crops and raised livestock for thousands of years before the invention of refrigeration, so curing and preserving foods of every sort are ancient arts. Through the ever-evolving science of agriculture, humanity has gone from barely subsisting to harvesting a great variety and abundance of crops.

Countless droughts and blights have led to as many famines. During the famous Irish Potato Famine of the 1840s; over a million people starved, yet that was far from history's worst agricultural disaster. Famine regularly ravaged ancient Mesopotamia, Egypt and China. In the twentieth century, famines claiming millions of lives struck Russia, China and India. A little less than a century ago, the United States suffered a terrible coincidence. The Stock Market crashed in 1929, and the rain stopped falling in the Midwest in 1931. In the midst of the *Dust Bowl*, on April 14, 1935, a great dust storm that started on what came to be known as *Black Sunday* traveled 2,000 miles all the way to Washington

D.C. and actually brought the problem to the U.S. capitol to influence the federal legislation that finally addressed the soil-erosion problem. After the stormy clouds had passed, the Soil Conservation Act was passed a week later on April 27, 1935. The Soil Conservation Service became a prominent branch of the Department of Agriculture. Unfortunately, many Midwestern farmers were not able to return to their farms.

Farm estates can draw income from five sources: the farm, the restaurant, the Village Inn, the farm-related cottage industries, and the rental income from residents who commute to work. With a diversified village economy owned by one hundred shareholders, estate families will never lose their farm. The fields, orchards and vineyards will be managed by an amalgamated union of agricultural entrepreneurs; professional and amateur; full-time and part-time. They will hedge their agricultural bets by growing the widest possible variety of crops.

With perspicacious stewardship of their natural resources, farm economies can weather economic downturns. If plenty of residents need work, the farm can switch to more labor-intensive crops. After the harvest, the farm can create work by processing their produce. During good times, the farm sells their apples. During not-so-good times, they cook apple sauce, press apple cider, and bake apple pies. Even in the worst of circumstances, residents will never starve, and they'll certainly never lack something to keep them busy. Beautiful farms can be developed into rich, family-friendly environments. Kids growing up on the farm might get mixed up with a bunch of swine, which is far better than being hustled by local gang-bangers cruising for recruits.

Picture amber waves of grain dancing in the wind under a bright blue sky. Autumnal orchards on moonlit nights glimmering with fireflies and buzzing with crickets. Starlight shimmering on frozen lakes on placid winter evenings. Romance aside, farming enterprises must be cultivators of true value so they can compete in the greater market outside of their idyllic, bucolic, rustic homesteads.

Your cutting-edge experimental farm will acquire seeds from around the globe. Once the seed search has begun and the invitation has been put forth, strange seeds will begin to arrive. Exotic seeds from the far reaches of the planet will show up at these Hollywood farms eager to audition in the soil. After a long journey, these seeds will be dying to play a part in an agricultural movie. A few of these experimental crops may end up playing a role in the local cuisine.

Farm estates should consider hosting a seed bank / agricultural support team / produce brokerage to help local free-lancers grow small crops on roof tops, empty lots and garden plots. The Seed Bank will distribute seeds proven to grow well in the local climate, and experimental seeds that show promise. Veteran farmers will guide novice agriculturalists every step of the way. Freelance farmers will have the security of knowing they can get the extra help they need come harvest time. If they're not inclined to hawk their produce in the fall, they can feel assured they will fetch a fair price selling their crop through the produce brokerage

Farm residents will be having so much fun—They'll just have to let people visit. Colorful roadside produce stands will lure curious travelers off the road. Visitors might expect an historical re-enactment of a colonial hamlet. What they will discover is a village—which may appear old-fashioned—yet will prove to be surprisingly modern. Definitely not Disneyland, but rather a real farm going about its business.

Visitors will soon realize that the multi-faceted experience they're witnessing is better than checking into a motel room and fighting over the remote or spending another boring night at the bowling alley. If hunger strikes, the restaurant stays open late. If they want to spend the night, the guesthouse is that big two-story building on the other side of the Village Green: the one with the wrought-iron balconies. There's also a secluded campground on the far side of the orchards.

Visitors will be visually impressed by a handsome village and prospering farm. Guests will be emotionally stimulated by friendly residents welcoming them everywhere they wander. Wayfarers will be intellectually aroused by the intriguing array of progressive farming methods on display. Last and certainly not least, travelers' taste buds will be seduced by delicious homespun culinary creations. With a cornucopia of fresh organic food, chefs and bakers will discover their paradise, so it's only natural to have a village restaurant and community bakery.

There are over a billion farmers in the world today. Most are subsistence farmers working their land with few of the advantages of modern farming technology. Struggling farmers worldwide are in need of fellowship. Corrupt governments oppress rural communities in two ways. In many places, small farmers are forced to sell out to big agribusiness and have little choice but to move to big metropolitan areas. In other places, small farmers are allowed to remain on their land but are impoverished by the oppressive policies of urban oligarchs. The mega-farms with the mega-machines have their place in a world with so many mouths to feed. Meanwhile, small-scale family farms everywhere should be dynamic, healthy and prosperous places to work and live.

Ten

The People's Corporation Grows

1.—The Rulebook

F or millions of carefree days, primitive people lived one day at a time, laying up nothing for the morrow. No laws, except the Laws of Nature. Unfortunately, such romantic characterizations of our ancient ancestors must be tempered by recalling how harsh Mother Nature can be. Imagine breaking your arm in the wild and being left to the primitive resources at hand.

Prehistoric people learned from their mishaps and failed escapades. Over succeeding generations, tribes developed precepts and codified precedents. The first human societies adopted rules based on their trials and travails—what to avoid, what to be on the lookout for, which actions benefited and which behaviors endangered the tribe. Ancient people established traditions to ensure their survival. Their ceremonies celebrated their mastery of a challenging natural environment.

Tribes developed methods to settle disputes to maintain harmony. Members who went astray had to face the consequences of their actions. Disputants appeared before their elders and were given a thorough hearing. When communities resolved a conflict, they searched for ways to discourage recurring problems from happening again. Elders named crimes and conceived matching punishments. Societies were practicing many forms of proto-law long before legislators wrote down laws, judges donned robes or municipalities built jails.

Often tribes had to go on living with lawbreakers, so penalties were conceived to rehabilitate rather than punish—not so tough as to destroy an offender's spirit, but harsh enough to convey their society's dissatisfaction. Starting more than 5,000 years ago, growing civilizations ushered in a new age of cruel and unusual punishments. Imperial rulers had far less patience and understanding than their primitive forebears. Researchers could fill volumes chronicling all the merciless punishments and tortures conceived since the dawn of civilization. Punishment was especially cruel for the poor who stole from the rich. While the less fortunate were brutally punished and tortured, their overlords remained above the law and could do as they pleased.

Ancient Rome developed a long train of legal traditions over a stretch of a thousand years before Roman Law was codified by Byzantine Emperor Justinian in the 6th century. Many legal terms retain their Latin wording (e.g. *habeas corpus, ad hoc, affidavit, alibi, prima facia, quid pro quo*, etc.). A major break with top-down tradition occurred in A.D. 1215 when the Magna Carta ceded power to the English Parliament and the seeds of the Enlightenment were planted. English Common Law developed from the legal precedents set by the high courts and parliamentary procedure over a period of more than a thousand years. Although the first religious laws enforced uniformity of belief, such prohibitions slowly gave way to religious tolerance, which eventually led to religious freedom. England's constitutional monarchy inspired the United States Constitution. Across Europe, Napoleonic Codes displaced the power of the church and the nobility, abolished feudalism and created uniform sets of laws that remain the foundation of many European legal systems.

Our modern legal system has been thousands of years in the making. The history, theory and practice of law may be fascinating, but unless you are a law student or involved in a legal dispute, the law is likely the last thing you want to think about. Lawyers are famous for the ire many of them rightly deserve, and most people have little appreciation for lawyers until they need one to get them out of a jam. People applaud the legal system when justice is done, then denounce it when they suspect a miscarriage of justice.

At one extreme, there are always a few rebels who believe the ultimate freedom is a world without rules, yet just what kind of life they hope to lead is hard to imagine. The purpose of rules is to preserve the harmony of the community by drawing boundaries and setting limits. Certain activities and behaviors may be prohibited while other activities are confined to certain places and times. Our enlightened society cannot rightly dictate to outsiders "you are not allowed to do that" before we have established a rule regarding that behavior supported by a reasonable justification for its prohibition or limitation.

Rule-making symposiums may create a strange role-reversal for members because it presents the rather odd task of imposing rules on ourselves. We each follow (consciously and unconsciously) a set of rules we have adopted based on our experiences and preferences, so we can observe within ourselves how rulemaking is inherent in human reasoning. Many people retain bad memories of legalistic knit-pickers who knew all the rules and spoiled all the fun. For the obsessive-compulsive adherent to the code, the rules come first, yet for most people, rules are the last thing they want to worry about most of the time.

When rules are imposed on people against their will—struggle, strife and revolt ensue. When we impose our own rules on ourselves—harmony is possible. Making rules for other people is easy, so as a member of a rule-making team, you must be extra careful to craft a simple set of rules everyone can easily abide by. Rules are important, yet they are certainly not the answer to everything. Rules tend to beget more rules. Let's be careful not to tie our hands with excessively restrictive or overly complicated regulations. Do not go rule-crazy and spoil the fun with too many. Most rules are plain common sense; and most of the time, good people will be behaving themselves unconcerned about any rules.

A people's-corporation charter is a social contract that seeks to balance competition and cooperation. Our members and our companies and estates aim to out-do—not un-do one another. People's corporations reserve the right to choose their members. Prospective members must be ready, willing and able to contribute and participate; therefore of a certain physical and intellectual ability, educational attainment and emotional maturity.

A people's corporation also reserves the right to expel members. If someone is harming the progress of the organization, it is well advised to take decisive action. A growing people's corporation should rid itself of troublemakers; no matter how wealthy, good-looking, clever or charming they may be. We must remember, if we exclude a stubborn soul, we are not banishing them into the wilderness. If anyone misrepresented themselves to get in the door then they have already broken the social contract of mutual honesty. Troublemakers got by just fine before they showed up at your door, and they will do just as fine after they are shown the door.

It is highly troubling when a group of talented entrepreneurs fights over their success rather than cooperating to make the most of it. It is also highly avoidable. When there's money involved in a business arrangement, all concerned parties need to draw up a contract that precisely defines what is expected of each participant and how they are to be compensated in every possible outcome. Regardless of the experience level of participants, contract law must prevail for a business system to function properly.

The centerpiece of a private, local justice system is a forum to settle disputes. A good private justice system aims to let offenders do their penance, pay their penalty, learn their lesson and move on as quickly as possible. The aim of settling disputes is to put disturbing matters to rest, once and for all. In many cases, a fair hearing will deflate simmering tensions and disperse confusing clouds of anger. In easy cases, the reconciled parties come to an agreement they both can live with. They will shake hands, walk away and be done with it. For difficult cases, judges will have to pass judgments and apply penalties.

The only way to create a crime-free society is to eliminate every incentive for criminal behavior. Local legal systems should investigate what inspired notable criminal behavior so they can fine-tune the corresponding social system. Deviant behavior should be traced to its origin and every effort made to eliminate all sources and incentives for crime.

2.–The General Company Grows

For a mature people's corporation with several dozen established estates, each estate sending a delegate to the General Council is the simplest way to organize representation. Representatives selected by their estate will have an interest in both halves of their economy: the household they live in and the firm they work for. Representation from home will allow all curious members to easily get involved in the governing process by attending the General Council as a stand-in or assistant.

Even if we do nothing malevolent and have nothing to hide, the public may still misperceive the corporation's actions, intentions and motives. Rumors have strange ways of spreading before you know it. The General Company needs to know what people on the street are saying about our "enlightened" organization. Our public relations should aim to make a good first impression without going overboard. No need to brag. No need to rag. No need for ads featuring suspiciously happy people dancing on countertops, or any exaggerated depiction of what we do. Let's do our best to foster a positive public image and counter any misperceptions.

We should establish a walk-in community center in a downtown location to engage directly with the public. With doors wide open to the passing public, community forums will satisfy the public's curiosity and invite their participation. As far as the community center's activities, a distinct line should be drawn between charitable activities for which no recompense is asked and funded programs for which a measurable return is expected. How about cooking and serving free meals? Go ahead and make them healthy and tasty. Make it a weekly affair if you like. Make it a daily affair if you can. Free flu shots? As long as you can afford to do it—Go right ahead. *Remember we must make money before we give it away.* You know there is a distinct value feeding hungry people good food. For our more substantial social investments, we want to find a way to measure the results of our efforts. For example, an after-school tutoring program's success can be measured by improvements in academic performance and classroom attendance.

Contributing to the community and earning an honest living will rightly grant your people's corporation status on the block. We will all be stakeholders—not speculators, yet we must be careful not to overplay our part. Never claim to be magicians with all the answers. Invite people to participate while letting them know that the magic can only happen by pioneering innovative methods, creatively over-coming obstacles and persistently working to achieve our mutual objectives.

3.–Marketplace

Retail companies that have grown to maturity in a Business Nursery are transplanted to permanent homes in a private-commonwealth marketplace—a sprawling, wide-spectrum shopping emporium on the outskirts of town. Such a marketplace of up to one hundred factory-stores is designed to be a dynamic working, marketing and educating environment where up to 1,000 tradespeople manufacture and market retail goods. A private-commonwealth marketplace will be an exciting destination for shoppers, aspiring artisans and curiosity seekers—more than a shopping mall and much like an amusement park.

Welcome to the People's Corporation Marketplace—a marketplace of the future, yet in so many ways a marketplace inspired by the past with blacksmiths, butchers, bakers and candlestick makers (silversmiths). Retail-manufacturing companies will be true factory outlets each with their own workshop, classroom and showroom. Rather than a cold, impersonal, fluorescently lit shopping mall, visitors will discover a warm, friendly, sunlit crafting and shopping environment.

A Private Commonwealth Marketplace can be so many things modern stores and malls are not: a vibrant and central feature of your urban landscape; a place that expresses the local culture; a place to gather, to learn, to have fun; and a place where tradespeople earn a good living. We can proceed to the Marketplace to learn how the world works by observing its economy in action.

During most trips to the local megastore or shopping mall, shoppers rarely have any meaningful contact with the sales staff. Custom and repair work is largely out of the question. Shoppers don't learn much about the products they purchase or meet any of the people who make what they buy. What one finds at the local megastore or shopping mall is very much the same as the next megastore or shopping mall down the road, and the next one. In a private-commonwealth marketplace, no one will feel like a stranger. It won't be about getting customers in and out as fast as possible or taking advantage of your guests with every gimmick in the book to get them to part with their money. If someone strolls in and wants to buy the whole store, they should be given special attention. Marketplace companies should be able to develop ways to cater to big spenders without sacrificing service to everyday clientele.

While strolling through the shopping wonderland, we can watch the woodworkers crafting beautiful furniture or observe skilled tailors sewing alluring clothing. Check out the chefs cooking sumptuous meals. When you get that I-want-to-do-that–!—I-want-to-learn-that–! urge, you can inquire about tours, classes and seminars. The Marketplace will be a go-to destination for older folks to pursue hobbies and young people to learn arts and crafts. Each company workshop will be a haven for lovers of their craft—a place where veteran artisans give curiosity seekers a first taste, help beginners advance their skills and (when they become available) offer talented diehards apprenticeship opportunities.

True factory-retail outlets, able to do custom work, can offer hundreds of choices rather than a few. Our mantra is: *diverse, flexible, creative.* Let's say you're in the market for a denim jacket. If you were searching through the local mall, you would find a limited selection. Private-commonwealth clothing emporiums, ready to do custom work, can offer a wide variety of fabrics and adornments. How about a leather collar? Would you consider some suede frills? Maybe some custom embroidery? Not quite feeling blue?—How about purple or turquoise denim?

By soliciting design ideas from creative clientele, customers get exactly what they want, and artisans learn what patrons are looking for. Creative customers can commission beautiful one-of-a-kind custom work, so they are happy with (as another example) their new dresser. That chest of drawers, being solid and well-made, might last a hundred years. Such a beautiful piece of furniture may even increase in value over time and become a treasured antique one day rather than being tossed in the trash during the next move.

The customer is not "always right." By educating clientele rather than taking advantage of their ignorance, private-commonwealth-marketplace companies will give customers the best value for their money. Truthful marketing is the ultimate consumer advocacy. A private-commonwealth marketplace will inform customers completely and take responsibility for what they produce. Well-informed consumers will appreciate the integrity of an open and informative marketplace. When they are fully confident they're getting their money's worth, happy customers will spend their next windfall at their nearest private-commonwealth marketplace.

4.–Local Education

High-quality education is the surest path to upward economic and social mobility, yet many students lose their grip and slip off the education ladder. Elementary education is the foundation of a society's prosperity, so one must find it strange how so many school systems are perpetually beleaguered with an array of problems such as juvenile crime, mental health difficulties, unruly classroom behavior, reliance on social media, spiraling costs, bullying, unhealthy food, bad teachers, incompetent principals, underfunded programs, *ad infinitum.* It seems so many of the woes of society are caused by the failure of our educational systems while so many of the glories of society are due to the achievements of education.

Childhood academic performance is a good predictor of social harmony and future economic growth. When our children attend school, pay attention and do their homework, so many social and economic problems can be avoided. We should do whatever it takes to establish a great elementary, middle and high-school education system. If a people's corporation is going to overspend on anything, we would be well-advised to dedicate a generous portion of our resources on the education of our children, adolescents and teens.

Students from dysfunctional homes bring their problems to school causing a lot of trouble for teachers and fellow students. Parents must do their job at home, so teachers can properly do their job at school. We must do everything we can to foster a cooperative relationship between parents and teachers. When strong families support struggling ones in their village communities, most of the negative domestic influences that lead to poor academic performance can be avoided.

If you serve a bland meal to your eager dinner guests, they will trudge through their plates dutifully consuming what they can stand while reluctantly muttering trite, polite, obfuscatory comments. If you serve up a tasty meal exploding with flavor, your guests will rave about your cooking more than you might care to hear. It's the same with teaching: it ranges from bland to delicious. A school is only as good as its teachers. There's no substitute for erudition and experience, yet great learners do not necessarily make great teachers. Insipid and uninspiring teachers are the bane of any education system and should be avoided, given another job, or let go. When classroom time is a drag, school becomes a real ho-hum affair. With solid, go-to, fire-up-your-imagination teachers, students will remain inspired to learn.

In old-fashioned schools, students were expected to sit up straight, pay attention and speak only after being called on. The boys all had short hair. The girls all wore skirts. Many schools still require uniforms. Modern schools are quite different. Nowadays if students are not actively participating in a lively class, they might as well stay home and stream educational programming. In old-fashion schools, students were discouraged from questioning authority. In modern schools, engaged students are encouraged to ask probing questions. Students are no longer seen as blank slates upon which to impress knowledge. Sorry to say it took so long to figure out, but students of every age have feelings, and there is a distinct emotional dimension to learning. Students need to be in the right frame of mind and heart to get the most out of classroom time.

At the end of their work day, good teachers enjoy the satisfaction of having taught many things to many curious young minds. At the end of their school day, enthusiastic students go to sleep relishing the satisfaction of having learned many new things. When students come home from a great day at school, it didn't happen by accident. After all, a school is a production company, akin to a theatrical production company. The only way to ensure a good production is vigorous preparation and rehearsals. Actors (teachers) rehearse their lines, directors (principals) fine tune their presentations and producers (administrators) make it all come together to put on a good show.

5.–Apprenticeship

School expenses add up fast: teacher salaries, administrator salaries, student transportation, building maintenance, keeping up with the latest technology and so on. The first good way to reduce the cost of education is to get as much of it out of the classroom as early in the educational process as possible. In apprenticeship programs, students gain real-world experience from a young age learning skills that will enable them to pursue diverse career paths. Shop apprentices will better appreciate the relevance of classroom theories when they experience them in action and apply them in their work. Let's not forget: apprentices earn their own spending money rather than having to nag their parents for an allowance. Most apprentices will be economically independent several years before their fellow students pursuing college degrees.

From ancient times until quite recently, most aspiring students learned their professions through an apprenticeship. Prior to the establishment of the first law school in America, the Litchfield [Connecticut] Law School, all law was taught through apprenticeships. The first chief justice of the United States, John Jay, learned the law by apprenticing at a law firm in New York for four years before he passed the bar. In days gone by, many apprentices endured slave-like conditions to learn their trade. Nowadays many tradespeople go through what may be called an apprenticeship, yet how much personal attention they actually receive varies widely. In a robust apprenticeship program, beginners are given a vital role in the production process while learning their trade. As their knowledge grows and their experience broadens, apprentices become more productive and their creativity is awakened.

Most high schools no longer require shop classes. Vocational schools now teach the trades. Many students are discouraged from pursuing a trade because they believe a traditional degree leads to better earning opportunities. It is a commonly held belief that people end up earning more money using their mind than working with their hands.

People worked with their hands for eons before they worked principally with their minds, and many accomplished people still make a living working with their hands. Traditional cultures encourage students to pursue both a vocational and an academic career to widen their employment opportunities and give them a balanced view of the world of work. Making stuff harkens back to the beginnings of craft tradition. Working with one's hands is soul-satisfying. Craftspeople make visible, tangible, one-of-a-kind things that beautify the world and bring people joy.

The white-collar–blue-collar divide is not the chasm many believe it to be. The wages of workers at the top of their trade easily rival the earnings of many college graduates. Wherever you go, plumbers earn more than librarians. Carpenters with ten or more years' experience who are willing to study on the side for a few years, become qualified general contractors. Exceptional tradespeople get promoted to foreman and the most ambitious are able to climb into the executive suite.

There is a gray area between what can rightly be called a trade and what can properly be considered a profession. Dance is a trade: dancers train in studios to prepare for stage productions. Acting is a trade after all. The difference is that dancers and actors train for years before they earn a dime, while shop apprentices can earn money from day one because they contribute to the production process. There is a gray zone between arts and trades. Only when it gets glamorous is it considered art. For example, let's say some woodworking artisans offer some ho-hum, seen-it-before furniture. That's craft. Then let's say some other, more inspired and sophisticated artisans display a roomful of dazzling, out-of-this-world home furnishings like-you've-never-er-seen-before... all of a sudden people consider such unique creations to be art.

By giving students the freedom to choose the vocations they pursue, they will have no one else to blame if their foray into the trades does not work out the way they hoped. It's good to learn new skills and give stuff a try in any case. So if a budding physicist is fascinated with auto mechanics, she can give it a go to find out if she really enjoys the knuckle busting and doesn't mind the grease. Developing a set of useful skills is time well spent, and when shop students go on to pursue academic careers, their experience in trade work will enrich their understanding of abstract principles. Over the long run those trade skills might come in handy. Let's say our curious mechanic does go on to study physics. She will certainly have a more practical understanding of machines in general and automobiles in particular.

It also needs to be said once again—Some kids are just not cut out for college and pursuing a trade is the most realistic ticket to success for them. By the time their contemporaries who followed an academic path return home with their undergraduate degrees, tradespeople will be starting their fifth year of shopwork. Learning a trade can be almost fool-proof. Shop-trade skills are taught in a very orderly sequence. Apprentices master one set of skills completely before they move on to the next. Apprentices who are slow-to-learn yet quick-to-remember who are allowed to progress at their own pace will never fall behind. Masters taking on apprentices gives novices the opportunity to learn their trade while supplying shop stewards with trusty helpers. Nothing gives a master more satisfaction than an apprentice who can be left on their own. Nothing gives an apprentice more confidence than being able to tackle their own projects from start to finish.

When an academic career comes to a standstill, a vocation becomes an alternative career path. When a vocational career starts to lag, students can pick up their academic pursuits where they left off, or academic and vocational careers can combine. Pursuing a business education while learning a trade enables graduates to master both their trade and the business of their trade. Aspiring engineering students apprenticing in our Industrial Park will gain practical knowledge that enriches their theoretical understanding. Computer-aided designs skills and shop-based fabricating skills are a good combination that balances the theoretical and the practical, the physical and the mental.

Learning for learning's sake and entertaining the brain with knowledge are wonderful ways to while away the time, yet students are looking to get their money's worth for all the years they invest in schoolwork, shopwork and fieldwork. An education data bank can keep precise records of every student's academic and vocational achievements, so they always know where they stand and what the prospects are in the fields they are pursuing.

6.–Industrial Park Development

A people's corporation's prosperity depends on its ability to produce a wide range of goods and services. Service-trade companies will do almost all their business within the city. Marketplace companies will do most of their business with locals, tourists and online customers. Industrial Park companies focus on goods for export and will do most of their business with wholesale customers outside the local economy. While Marketplace companies grow by continually widening their product lines, Industrial Park companies grow by focusing on a specialty. The Industrial Park might become a showcase for cutting edge, highly unusual production techniques making bizarre stuff few people know about with machines few people have laid their eyes on.

There are several ways Industrial Park companies can cooperate. Metal-fabricating companies mold, machine and stamp metal parts to supply makers of kitchen appliances, bicycles, tools and motor vehicles. Other parts-making companies supply a wide array of parts to a series of finished-goods makers. Several companies can produce a line of goods marketed under a single brand name. Consider a kitchen-equipment conglomerate: one company makes espresso machines, another stoves, another utensils, another refrigerators.

Several companies can form an assembly line to produce complex machines. Consider a small, boutique scooter manufacturing conglomerate of five companies. The first company fabricates the frames and body panels—the second company specializes in engines—the third in transmissions—the fourth in electrical systems—all delivered to the fifth company: the assembly company. Swank Marketplace showrooms could feature the wares of Industrial Park conglomerates like the scooter makers. Marketplace companies could be part of an Industrial Park assembly line. Retailers, tradespeople and manufacturers regularly gather to explore every possible way they can cooperate developing and marketing new products.

Industrial Park apprenticeship programs work closely with the High School and the University. Engineering students gain experience working with machines before designing or re-engineering them. Electrical engineering students gain valuable experience working as electricians and technicians. Mechanical engineering students get their hands dirty working as (you guessed it) mechanics and technicians.

Theoretical knowledge combined with hands-on experience will fortify students' passion to excel—to become—in due time—masters of the industrial universe.

Ambitious industrialists set aside time for tinkering and brainstorming. The human mind conceives fresh ideas by drawing on its knowledge. The more a mind knows, the more novel ideas it can synthesize. Industrial knowhow is enhanced by reading the journals, going to the conventions and learning how other companies in the industry handle their business. Since private-commonwealth industrial companies cannot be the biggest, they should aim to be knowledgeable and capable enough to pioneer a profitable niche in the local and regional market.

If an industrial company expresses interest in a million-dollar machine, a very eager salesperson will soon show up at their door ready to tell them all about it. Industrial-machine makers only earn money if their clients make money with their machines. It is wholly in the interest of industrial-machine makers to support their customers every step of the way.

When an industrial company ships their first orders, they do not want their customers to be disappointed. Cultivating happy customers is their number one priority. After going to so much trouble to make and market their goods, they strive to cultivate a steady clientele. Dealing with other industrial companies is a whole other ballgame than selling to retail customers who are often too lazy to return something they bought on a whim and were not happy with. Manufacturers and retailers employ professional buyers, quality inspectors and shipping clerks who will not hesitate to return components that fail to meet their specifications.

Industrial marketing is straightforward. Industrial suppliers know will be dealing with sane, sober, level-headed production supervisors who need precise information to make their purchasing decisions—not buckets full of babbling ballyhoo and mindless slogans. This can be refreshing both when it comes to interpreting suppliers' marketing and developing your own. Just keep in mind that in manufacturing, it's rarely about crafting a stylish image or promoting some sort of mystique around what you do.

How does an industrial company excel? Consider a machine shop. Every machine shop purchases their lathes, milling machines, grinders and blocks of steel, aluminum and titanium from more or less the same suppliers as their competitors. To succeed, a manufacturing company producing a generic product or providing a common service must be at least as efficient at managing their resources as their competitors. Efficiency can only be stretched so far—Creativity and innovation are the x-factors that can really boost earnings. To excel, a company must be able to do stuff other companies can't do. When a manufacturer develops a unique industrial process, they can earn licensing revenues from their patented processes. When a manufacturer pioneers a unique line of products that turns out to be a hit, they can command premium prices.

With thousands of bicycle riders, our municipality will be able to support a bicycle industry. Most bicycle makers weld the frames and forks that bear their brand name and outsource the rest of the components. Local bicycle makers should master welding frames and forks before tackling the more challenging task of fabricating components. Bicycle components: brakes, derailleurs, sprockets and chains, may be subject to patent restrictions, so market opportunities and intellectual property issues should be thoroughly researched. With the bike factory in the back pumping out a new model every few days, the retail shop in the front will be able to display an impressive array of creatively designed and colorfully-detailed bicycles. In addition to servicing the machines they sell, retail bike shops will also be able to offer a full range of services for all bicycles.

Looking to future growth, bicycle mavens keep in mind how the first airplanes, automobiles and motorcycles were developed with bicycle technology: the Wright Brothers were bicycle mechanics. Henry Ford built his first automobiles with bicycle parts. Harley and Davidson began their company building motor-bicycles.

To master the ways and means, you must master machines. Welcome to the industrial amusement park. By all means, the Industrial Park should show off their machines. Machines as big as buildings. Machines that fit in the palm of your hand. Picture spectators strolling along catwalks above a series of factory floors. Curious visitors peer down upon a menagerie of wild machine beasts caged on the floor below. There are a lot of lonely machines that would appreciate some good company: big machines, mean machines growling and grinding, bizarre contraptions you never knew existed until you laid your weary eyes on them. Spellbound spectators descend to the factory floor to stroll along designated pathways to witness machines grinding, binding, unwinding, conveying, lifting, crushing, heating, cooling, spooling, melting, smelting, molding, pressing, injecting, detecting and perfecting.

Eleven

Private-Commonwealth Municipality

1.–Cityhood

T he idea of pioneering a sovereign political realm in a remote rural location is far-fetched indeed. Far more difficult to do than imagine—of course—yet there's no harm in dreaming bigger and bolder than ever before. A people's corporation can be started with relatively modest resources. A private-commonwealth municipality is a more complicated and costly venture that will require tens of millions of dollars to start and hundreds of millions of dollars to complete. City pioneers must be careful—because if they bet big—they can lose big. A private-commonwealth municipality is best pursued by one or more successful people's corporations with enough chutzpah, capital and human momentum to take on such an immense and daunting project.

This is where the pieces of the puzzle come together to form the ultimate whole. First, I presented a way to pursue happiness in the workplace by earning a good living in a promising career. Then I described how to create a rich living environment to enjoy happiness at home. Next, I outlined the diversified and integrated economic dynamo of a people's corporation operating in a small city. Now, let's reassemble those pieces on a raw parcel of land of several square miles for the ultimate actualization of local harmony.

We will not be heading to Washington D.C. to mount a massive public protest to challenge the prevailing political order. Rather, we will venture in the opposite direction to a sparsely populated countryside to break ground on a civilization of our own design. As private-commonwealth municipality founders, we will be trailblazing an economic, social, political and spiritual frontier. We are determined to remain emancipated from the prison of stifling ideas that left us living half the life we could be living before we learned to live in harmony.

The roots of the word *democracy* are demos (meaning people) and cracy (meaning power). Democracy literally means *people power*. Good democracies harness the power of all the people, not just those with power and influence. Democracy is not the most natural form of government. Long ago, when the first settled societies needed order, clever and ambitious leaders took charge. People fell in line and order was established. Over time, the leaders' power went to their heads. They took more than their fair share and after common people figured out they were being taken advantage of, they inevitably sought to even the score.

Establishing a true democracy can be likened to the mass production of aluminum (It's an unusual analogy, but it works). Aluminum doesn't exist naturally in its metallic state. The first extraction method produced the first aluminum in 1856, but it was extremely expensive. For several decades, aluminum was a precious metal more valuable than gold. Skeptics insisted it would be impossible to produce on a large scale. Once a cost-effect way to produce aluminum came on line in 1886, the world had a rustproof, lightweight, flexible metal with hundreds of uses. Similarly, establishing the first true democracy in the modern world will take a lot of trial and error, but once it's accomplished, we can live in lightweight, rustproof, flexible, open, equal and fair governments. Once local, small-scale, true democracies are established, the world will have a formula to follow and a model to imitate. People will be inspired to join in where it is happening or make it happen where they are.

A true democracy is the precise opposite of a cult. Cult followers are drawn to a charismatic leader. Seekers drawn to the democratic adventure described in this book are concerned, frustrated and adventurous people ready to go to great lengths to change their lives and change the world. Cult leaders assume people are dimwitted and prefer to be manipulated. Democratic leaders assume people are smart enough to make their own decisions. Cult leaders do their best to rule for life and determine their succession. Democratic leaders are elected by the people and hold power for a limited term at the pleasure of the people. Cults weaken democracies by mis-educating their followers and limiting their freedom. Democracies educate their constituencies so they are knowledgeable enough to enjoy a great degree of freedom.

2.–Civilization Design

A self-sufficient municipality in a remote location should be able to sustain itself if it gets cut off from the outside world. Let's not kid ourselves—we'll need an emergency plan: enough stored water, provisions and fuel to last thirty days or more; and most importantly, well-kept backcountry trails to the nearest highway.

This thought-experiment of designing a small city in a remote location gives us an engaging framework to re-examine, re-organize and synthesize a broad spectrum of knowledge toward a single purpose. Civilization design synthesizes many fields of study: architecture, urban planning, political science, economics, sociology, water-supply management, soil science and energy systems.

Many ancient civilizations such as Sumer, Egypt, the Incas and most famously Greece were amalgamations of city-states. Private-commonwealth municipalities are akin to independent city-states, yet are fully integrated with the greater world and kindred municipalities. Ancient city-states were unequal in size and wealth and the stronger ones naturally dominated. Private-commonwealth municipalities are equal in scale and cooperate rather than vie to dominate one another.

The largest, most pristine and least-expensive rural properties on the market are not located near big cities or major highways. They're at the end of long-and-lonely roads leading to the "middle of nowhere." The middle of nowhere is somewhere of course. They just call it that because no one's living there—yet. Adventurers will be drawn to the wildest locations because of their enormous size and unparalleled beauty.

Every type of terrain has advantages and disadvantages. Mountainside land (full of rocks and trees) is significantly more expensive to develop than prairieland where trees are sparse and rocks are few. Agricultural opportunities are limited in the mountains. Narrow north-south valleys receive only a few hours of direct sunlight each day. What can be grown commercially depends on the amount of bottom-land. Rural properties sell at prices based on the expected return from their natural resources, so productive forest and farmland are more expensive than craggy mountain and arid desert properties. The easily-cultivatable natural resources developers spend extra for in the beginning will likely be worth it over the long run. Uninhabited islands require infrastructure upgrades in water, transportation, sanitation and energy just to make them habitable. The added expense of running a small fleet of boats would put island industries at a disadvantage. If developers have their hearts set on an island, they should find one they can eventually build a bridge to. An estate could pioneer an island resort, but it is best not to venture too far from shore.

The greatest drawback of remote properties is their distance from the nearest cities. The farther away a private-commonwealth municipality is located, the higher the transportation costs and the greater the resources needed to persuade curiosity seekers to visit. A rail line connecting a remote city to the outside world would make that settlement more feasible by significantly reducing the transportation costs for goods and increasing the convenience and quality of transportation for people.

Throughout the North American continent, the heartland is vast and varied. Unusual parcels of land will present both unique challenges and distinct opportunities. Out west, vast tracks of relatively inexpensive barren land (e.g. tundra, scrubland, badlands, lava fields) are available, yet developers must devise a scheme to surmount the challenges of the land's limitations. If water can be accessed, desert land can be transformed into an oasis. In arid regions that have an extended rainy season, harvesting and storing rainwater in enormous cisterns would provide substantial water supplies. An enormous subterranean reservoir fed from a remote mountain water source could sustain a desert metropolis. Greenhouses diffuse harsh sunlight and conserve limited water supplies. Badlands may be ideal for massive solar- and wind-farms large enough to power an entire city.

Farmland is the easiest terrain to work with because it's already been cleared and flattened. On farmland or prairieland, a boomtown can be built in no time. Most Kansas and Nebraska farms are owned by large holding companies that will (for the right price) sell vast tracks. A system of canals requires grading land perfectly flat. The dirt removed to excavate canals and lakes can be used to build hills. Adding crushed rock and demolished concrete to the dirt would increase the size and structural strength of hills while improving drainage.

Suitable properties can be found in the listings of national rural-real-estate dealers. A real-estate development gone bust could be a golden opportunity. In urban and suburban areas, occasionally defunct private and public institutions, such as failed shopping malls or decommissioned airports and military bases do come on the market.

Establishing a brand new city in a remote location will inspire resourcefulness, improvisation and originality leading to a unique local culture. It's hard to say at the beginning how it will all turn out in the end. What will your town be famous for? A unique cheese? An annual music festival? A world-renowned physics department? You never know.

3.—True Democracy

The formation of small-scale, true democracies that achieve high standards of living will be one of the pinnacles in the ascent of humankind. Naysayers will claim it can't be done; yet once it is accomplished, bystanders will be wondering why it took so long and they'll be looking for great things to come from it.

How the democratic government of a private-commonwealth municipality works is rather straightforward. Estates govern their neighborhood affairs in estate councils. Each estate appoints a representative to attend the General Council. Each representative has an interest in an estate and a share in a company. The General Council of one hundred representatives crafts the policies that shape the character and culture of the municipality. These assemblies of direct representatives will possess the common trust because they share the same interests as their constituents and are directly affected by the policies they personally implement.

In the United States of America, elected officials swear an oath to uphold the Constitution. In a private-commonwealth municipality, every member will *also* swear an oath that affirms their commitment to the common cause. Passionate participation in government at the local level will harness the full brainpower of the people toward governing their society.

In a small-scale direct democracy, there will be few full-time politicians. Being a local representative, who has regular personal contact with all their constituents, should be an easier job than representing a largely unknown constituency sprawled over an extensive territory. Taking on the vocation of representative will be a parallel career pursued by members with the appropriate experience and education.

Graduate-level educators specialize in teaching, researching and investigating. The general government of a private-commonwealth municipality would require an enormous amount of researching and investigating into all aspects of local life to do their job, so it makes sense for the upper levels of the education system and the general government to integrate their efforts. It's a good match because it brings together people thinking about stuff with people doing stuff, and balances theoretical learning with the practical application of that theory to running a government immediately at hand. Democratic leaders will inform their constituents of the situation rather than wasting their time with empty rhetoric. Teachers and students can collaborate on issues of mutual interest or concern. University students earn college credit through internships, apprenticeships and regular attendance at the General Council. Current affairs will be the talk of the town beginning at the General Council and continuing in corner cafés, classrooms and living rooms all over town.

The *Key to Paradise*—Banish bad information. The simple solution to dishonesty in government is to hold government officials to the same academic standards as professors and students. The first order of business, today and every day, is to get your facts straight. Officials will be required to validate questionable information, cite sources and defend the use of any controversial research they use to justify their proposals.

Instead of mastering fancy vituperation and bitter partisan debating techniques, representatives will master the art of discussing issues with good humor and zeal. Representatives will passionately propound cohesive arguments and present concise analyses rather than parroting talking points crafted to disguise special interests. Instead of a war of wills, representatives will dialog with a spirit of openness and cooperation.

The private-commonwealth governing system eliminates the conflicts of interest between the wealthiest and poorest members of society. Every member of the municipality will have a place to live, full access to work opportunities, education and healthcare. No person or company will have any incentive to act against the common interest. There will be no lobbyists or influence peddlers currying favor for their pet projects. Everyone and anyone will be able to walk through the front door to take care of their business. Nobody will have to sneak through the back door to "really get things done."

In true democracies, the people live, work and govern together. In authoritarian governments, the ruling class lives apart from the people. In authoritarian oligarchies, the upper classes send their children to elite schools and do their best to conserve their advantages. In true democracies, every youngster attends the same elementary, middle and high schools. Authoritarian governments tend to emphasize the masculine virtues of aggression, exertion and domination. True democratic equalarchies thrive on a balance between masculine and feminine qualities. Authoritarian governments operate on a double standard. In a true democracy, the double standard is dead, no one is above the law and the highest officials are held to the highest standards.

The private-commonwealth governing model resolves most of the shortcomings of compromised democracies. In large-scale democracies, the attention is drawn to a strong war of wills in which the priority is winning the ideological argument rather than crafting the best solution. The private-commonwealth political system eliminates long, drawn-out and costly election campaigns. In such a small-scale system, voters will have a chance to meet candidates for citywide officials in person. Instead of a popularity contest played out through a media war, a series of public debates and interviews will allow members to choose the best applicant for the job.

4.–City Design

City living remains popular. For better or for worse, more people move to cities every day. Many historians celebrate the city as one of humankind's greatest achievements. Herein we reinvent the city by conceiving a fresh, updated, turbocharged model city able to thrive far into the future. Civilization designers can draw inspiration for their model city by recalling the city they grew up in, studying the cities they have lived in and comparing the thousands of noteworthy cities that have arisen since civilization began.

Once a private-commonwealth municipality breaks ground; designers, landscapers and construction crews will set up elaborate camps: one for working and another, a significant distance away, for living. Breaking ground will be a down-and-dirty, rough-and-tumble affair. Everyone involved will meet on a regular basis to coordinate their activities and compare their observations. Outsiders will be curious about such an epic project in a remote location. Our journalists can share their impressions and conduct interviews to chronicle the progress of the grand project. Outside journalists will be instructed to bring camping gear and welcomed at the journalists' encampment.

The daily news focuses on current events, breaking news and the ongoing developments of unfolding stories. The news media seldom contemplates the big picture of the human condition. Any focus on the long-term prospects for humanity usually yields pessimistic predictions. Most commercial news outlets earn their money selling advertising designed to encourage consumption. Any realistic plan to save the planet will require curbing consumption. Doom-and-gloom predictions generally do not put the public in a buying mood, so most commercial news media avoids focusing on perennial issues that threaten the wellbeing of humanity and the future of life on Planet Earth.

Consider the ever-growing human population. More people on a limited planet leaves less resources for each person. Growing populations consume more, pollute more and strand more people struggling at the bottom. Swelling populations crowd cities, congest highways and strain infrastructure and public services. Growing populations are more likely to fight over scarce resources. With more people living in swelling shantytowns and festering favelas; landslides, earthquakes and tsunamis claim ever-larger death tolls.

Uncontrolled urban growth has spoiled many cities. People move from the hinterlands to enjoy the dynamism and pursue the opportunities of growing cities. Expanding populations crowd the inner city and encroach on its edges. Longtime residents grow discontent as their once-tranquil havens grow overcrowded. In rapidly growing cities; older, charming, working-class neighborhoods grow more expensive every year so longtime residents can barely afford the higher rents or fancy restaurants.

On the outskirts of town, farms and forests are sacrificed for suburban growth. Frustrated city dwellers move to the suburbs to escape the urban mayhem. In the city center, buildings rise higher, more people squeeze in, foot and automobile traffic swells. Affordable housing gets farther away from well-paying jobs. More people commute longer distances, creating congestion and increasing air pollution. To accommodate a growing army of commuters; bridges, tunnels, rail lines and subways are built and roads are widened.

Rather than an unplanned city of unlimited growth, it makes sense to limit the population of a planned city. Limiting the population preserves the quality of life built into the original design. There will be no need to enlarge, widen or rebuild any infrastructure if the city is built properly to begin with and the number of inhabitants is kept within the bounds of the capacity it was planned for. Designing a city with a set population makes the amount of space dedicated to each person and each activity precise considerations.

City planners consider the terrain they have to work with. Flat land is unencumbered by hills and unconstrained by the width of a valley. An oddly shaped parcel of property or hilly terrain challenges designers to conceive the optimal orientation of the city districts. Rivers can be an attractive natural feature and a productive resource. Rivers come with one big problem: they flood. Provisions for diverting a rapid rise in the water level should be incorporated into the master city plan. Planners develop most of the city on high ground, concentrating parkland and agriculture in the floodplain or building a canal or tunnel able to divert floodwaters.

Tall buildings conserve open land and create panoramic views from upper stories. Multi-use facilities make the best use of limited space, such as a theatre that can be used for movies, plays, concerts, lectures and ceremonies. Once city designers map out the land they have to work with, they can begin landscaping. They should do their best to conserve the most attractive features of the terrain. They should cut down as few trees as possible and plant as many as possible.

In mountainous country abounding in wood, stone and clay, readily-available natural building materials will inspire local architectural styles. Some of the strongest building wood grows in the Rocky Mountains: lodgepole pine and

Douglas fir. These trees were used to build rustic log cabins in the pioneer days and huge timber lodges in the decades to follow. The Rocky Mountains live up to their name. There are plenty of beautiful rocks on the mountain slopes to build and decorate with. In the valleys between mountain ranges, one can find an assortment of clays in flat streambeds.

The city should be open for business as soon as possible. Prudent city planners aim for the greatest beauty in the long run, but prioritize building basic infrastructure. City developers must not squander resources on magnificent monuments to their greatness before they can afford (or rightly deserve) them. Each city district should maintain a consistent architectural theme, while estates are encouraged to build bold and unusual. Once master builders lay out the basic road network, planners can design-as-they-go, filling in missing pieces based on insights and inspirations from everyone who has an opinion about it and shows up for the consequential planning meetings.

City developers do their best to design a beautiful and safe city with plenty of attractions for visitors—shopping, live music, cinema, theater, indoor and outdoor recreation, tours, seminars, healing centers, conventions, festivals and worship services. For music festivals, an expansive grass meadow in the Central Park is landscaped into a sylvan arena for summer concerts. Designers determine the maximum feasible number of visitors to make sure there is enough lodging and camping for the largest possible influx of people. Satisfied visitors will promote the city and its venues. Residents will prosper from the extra income and enjoy the facilities, events and curious visitors made possible by a healthy tourist economy.

In a small city in which the longest distance one has to travel is under a mile, it makes sense to do away with motor vehicles as the dominant mode of transportation. Within the city, people can get around on foot, bicycle, skate and skateboard. An automobile-free city would have a large parking lot outside the city walls. Residents and visitors pass through a welcome center to enter the city. For visitors this would resemble passing through customs when entering a foreign country. For cities located at the end of a road with *one way in* and *one way out*, everyone passes through the Welcome Center to enter the city. For cities on or near a highway, the city develops a Main Street Shopping District. Visitors patronize the Shopping District to get a feel for the city before passing through the Welcome Center.

The ideal path for a scenic roadway would be a circuit running completely around and along the outer edge of the city. It can be called the *Ring Road*, the *Beltway* or the *Panoramic Road*. By locating a principal transit route close to the perimeter, it will make for a grand tour of the city giving first timers a thorough overview of the metropolis. On special occasions, it can be used as a racecourse. Visitors can easily embark on a grand tour with no fear of getting lost. They can take a quick run through in about an hour or spend the whole day stopping off to tour the Marketplace, University, Industrial Park and Capitol Plaza.

Canoes and paddleboats traversing a system of canals provide a fun and relaxing mode of exercise and transportation. Canals can never be an after-thought or add-on. A system of canals must be built into the original city. Let Venice, Italy be an inspiration—then add irrigation, swimming, ice-skating and aquaculture to your grand local vision. Canals water tall trees and lush gardens. Paths cross waterways over idyllic stone-arch bridges. Under buildings, canals pass through long, brightly-lit tunnels eventually emerging in the middle of town to meander down magnificent reflecting pools leading from marketplaces to main plazas. During the construction of the city, flat-bottom barges pulled along canals would provide very efficient transportation for equipment and materials.

Great city parks are natural havens that provide a quick escape from the urban environments surrounding them. Residents will enjoy the scenery of the central park on their way to work or school. Aficionados of various sports can set up playing fields. Revelers bring their guitars, flutes and percussion instruments for jam sessions and drum circles. Those looking to cool off take a swim in the lake. Where the park borders the university campus, athletic fields and organized sporting companies make their home.

When we espouse "smaller government," we are not suggesting shrinking the magnificent municipal, state and federal buildings gracing American cities. In a great city, one expects a grand city hall and an impressive civic plaza. A building's size and magnificence proclaim its power and importance. The meeting hall I am envisioning is a circular chamber designed to accommodate one hundred representatives and one hundred assistants on the floor with seating for several hundred spectators in a viewing gallery above. A fully circular gallery leaves no place for a traditional stage. A gap in the gallery would increase the total floor space and leave a large recess for a stage.

The Capitol Plaza is where members go to take care of business with their public service companies. At the head of the Plaza is the Roundhouse I just described. On one side of the Plaza is the Municipal Office Complex housing the Municipal Bank, the Investment Company, the Commonwealth Insurance Company, the City Services Company and the Commonwealth Court. On the other side of the Capitol Plaza could be any variety of institutions: Pick two or three: a theatre (opera house),a luxury hotel, an estate apartment tower, a museum, a temple perhaps.

In a private-commonwealth municipality, there will be no multilayered bureaucracy to refuse or confuse citizens. The people will have direct access to all the administrators affecting their lives. If members have a problem with their insurance, they visit the Commonwealth Insurance Company to talk with an agent. Trouble with your estate's garbage pickup? There'll always be someone who can straighten out the situation right inside City Services.

Building a tall building in the middle of nowhere may seem out of place, yet please reconsider the idea for a minute. Multistory buildings reduce the overall footprint of buildings on the land. Every square foot of space you build on a second, third or higher floor is one less square foot you have to build elsewhere. In flat country, towers will be visible from miles around. Let's settle for a commanding sixteen-story tower with an upscale hotel on the upper stories with a rooftop viewing area (with restaurant, bar, an intimate stage) offering a grand view of the metropolis and surrounding countryside. Welcome: this is a great spot to start your evening. Behold the bustling marketplace, throngs of people strolling down romantic pathways, bicycle boulevards with a bewildering array of colorful cycles of every sort. Check out the glorious Central Park gleaming in the center of the tableau. The setting sun and rising moon beckon nighttime revelers to the various entertainment districts as the sun sets over the mountains.

5.–University Design

A people's corporation operating in a small city would develop educational facilities all over the city, suburbs and countryside. A private-commonwealth municipality on one large piece of property should set aside a choice parcel of land to centralize its educational facilities. Since the Middle Ages, prominent universities have prided themselves on their magnificent lecture halls, elegant courtyards and inspiring libraries. A private-commonwealth university could never rival the scope and grandeur of campuses such as Oxford or Harvard, yet they can develop an impressive enclave where budding poets can mingle with aspiring physicists.

Perhaps the term *university* is a little pretentious for the rather small institution envisioned here, yet private-commonwealth universities aim for a universal approach to teaching a wide spectrum of studies. Attractive remote campuses would attract outside students. Campuses close to metropolitan areas would attract commuting students. Adjacent private-commonwealth municipalities could combine resources to co-develop a university.

Rather than get lost in describing the landscaping, let's begin with the well-being of the student body. At the heart of the University is a lively educational resource center providing abundant advising and counseling services. Students will always have someone to discuss their goals, aspirations and challenges with. Good guidance, informed by accurate job forecasts, will give students a clear idea of the likely outcome of their schoolwork and the added rewards for exceptional academic performance.

Unfortunately, there is no secret stash of genius juice struggling students can imbibe from a cosmic chalice to boost their intelligence quotient. When learners progress at their own pace, learning becomes more fun, relevant and satisfying. Fast learners who excel at traditional schoolwork will likely set their sights on academic careers. High academic achievers are understandably proud of their accomplishments and many take pleasure flaunting their erudition to those who care to listen.

Many high school and college graduates are glad never to set foot in a classroom ever again. Other graduates pine for the classroom so the university should do their best to grant the perpetually curious every opportunity to continue their formal education. The university should host regular forums where curious students and visitors converse with educators. In such symposiums, concerned attendees ask their pressing questions and express their inspired observations. Such forums will enhance the public role of local professors and keep them in touch with what people are concerned with and fascinated by. Such public forums will inhibit the spread of misinformation, strengthen the organic social network and, if deemed newsworthy by the court of public opinion, inspire a lively public dialogue throughout the city.

A wise society recognizes, cultivates and rewards experts. A council of local experts can form a Guardianship or Illuminati of sorts. Most experts will be university professors, veteran journalists and elder members who have demonstrated an extraordinary degree of knowledge and wisdom: native savants if you will. A careful chronicling of each expert's track record can be used to scrutinize the reliability of their advice and the accuracy of their diagnoses and prognostications. Experts will be called on when their expertise is needed in government debates, settling disputes and brainstorming issues. Experts can write columns in local media outlets. Experts can go tête-á-tête in lively public debates concerning vital issues. The strange thing about expertise and wisdom is how formal education is a good predictor of standing in a club of the super-smart, but it's by no means totally reliable. People who have graduated from the School of Hard Knocks can be very wise people: call it native wisdom. Once you tap people for their wisdom, they will be encouraged to cultivate that knowledge and wisdom. A local Guardianship will inspire the quest for knowledge and wisdom throughout the society.

A private-commonwealth municipality is already in the education business, so hosting visiting students would boost the size and scope of the University. Visiting students would make up for the absence of members pursuing degrees in outside institutions. Hosting 500 to 1,000 students for two sixteen-week semesters is a substantial imposition, but it does leave twenty weeks of the year without the major influx of students. Even the most robust small university will be woefully underequipped to issue a full range of undergraduate degrees. Outside students will either do a visiting semester or attend to complete a degree offered by the University. Local students can do their first semester or full year of college at the University before transferring to outside undergraduate programs.

A new way of doing business calls for a school teaching that new way of doing business. Call it the *School for Sustainable Business*, (Humorists will dub it the *Institute of Lovenomics*) a school teaching how people can prosper without exploiting the natural environment or one another. Local color and history will come to influence much of the social-science curriculum. Elder professors might enjoy a cushy slot in an idyllic setting to spend their golden years. Whatever they introduce to the curriculum that enough students are interested in will add to the upper-level academic offerings.

Visit some beautiful university campuses to inspire your design. My favorite is Cornell University located in the beautiful lakefront city of Ithaca, New York. Cornell has a great combination of traditional and modern buildings on a rugged landscape famous for its spectacular gorges. There are hundreds of beautiful university campuses in the United States and thousands throughout the world from which to draw inspiration.

6.–Information System

There comes a point in the development of most prospering societies when the head starts to bite the tail. The people at the head want to stay at the head, so they do their best to misinform the less fortunate members of their society to keep them in their place. This regressive practice distorts the transmission of knowledge, stagnates social and economic progress and reinforces class divisions. The greatest prosperity is achieved by promoting a vigorous education system and providing equal opportunity to all members. With fair-minded leaders and a full-service education system, the head won't be biting its tail, the head will be busy doing its job leading an enlightened society to a bright future.

Healthy democracies feature a lively press that keeps the public informed. Dictatorships suppress free speech and promote propaganda. Conscientious elected officials and business leaders welcome intelligent criticism as part of the job and a source of inspiration to do a better job. Dishonest leaders depend on a misinformed or disinterested public. Cheaters dislike criticism, deny the truth, fight the truth tellers and do what they can to suppress freedom of the press. If the truth sets people free, then falsehoods keep people oppressed. Misleading information wastes people's time because when someone comes to believe a falsehood, to get things straight again they have to unlearn that falsehood and relearn the truth. If knowledge is power, then ignorance weakens and distorts power. If you don't know much—you can't do much. If you don't know where you're going—you can't get very far. Misinformation robs people of their peace of mind, destroys their common sense and leaves them unable to intelligently discuss current affairs or constructively participate in the running of their society.

Once a fledgling people's corporation is holding regular meetings, they should publish a journal to chronicle their progress. Members who miss meetings can read the journal to keep up with developments. Newcomers can study the journals to familiarize themselves with what took place before they arrived. The insights from observations chronicled by journalists will be used to improve every part of the society and economy. Comments on blog posts by people who participated in particular meetings will enrich the historical record.

A free press is vital to a free society. Just think of all the scandals journalists have uncovered over the years. This leaves sensible people to wonder why press freedom is so vulnerable. What endangers freedom of the press are the people and organizations that do not want their corrupt practices scrutinized or their dirty deeds exposed. The biggest distraction in the public sphere is the war of words now dominating popular discourse more than ever. There are still wolves at every gate and dirty players aplenty in the news game.

In due time, the journalists establish a journalism company to consolidate their efforts and coordinate their publications and broadcasts. Up to ten journalists choose their beat: local politics, local business, the local economy, university affairs, estate affairs, industrial-park affairs, entertainment, sports and human interest. With a private local news outlet, shareholders can focus on local news, local celebrities and local trends. Each estate will continue to publish a newsletter, which the estate reporter studies to summarize neighborhood affairs. Once they have a large enough readership, listenership and viewership; the journalists should be able to claim a reasonable salary. Only by producing media with a large outside following would a journalism company be able to turn much of a profit. There is always a demand for well-presented summaries of the day's news. Journalists might try their hand at news aggregation by producing vigorously fact-checked encapsulations of state, national and global news so viewers can keep up with current events without wasting hours a day watching dozens of YouTube channels.

I interpret the oft misquoted phrase "Where ignorance is

bliss—'tis folly to be wise" to be an eloquent way of saying there's no use speaking truth to ignorant people. Ignorance can be beneficial in certain rare cases. Imagine yourself on a plane that is going to crash in an hour. You would certainly enjoy that final hour of your life a lot more if you had no foreknowledge of the impending disaster. People have a tendency to ignore what they want to avoid—Why deal with something if you don't have to right now? I know most people worry too much and plenty of problems take care of themselves, yet in a complicated information-driven world; overall, it is to one's advantage to keep up with the latest. Ignoring information of consequence is rarely a good choice. Ignorance can be bliss for a brief while, but certainly not over the long run.

The next best thing to the Internet is a mini-Internet: a local-area network that ensures the private, secure and accurate exchange of data throughout the city. There's no reason to send information halfway around the world when it's only going a few blocks away. While the Internet can be compared to a ghetto with unsavory characters on every street corner, a properly managed local-area computer network will be like a classy town with safe neighborhoods supporting honest businesses with a bustling marketplace and vibrant town square. Members will be able to access the Internet as they need, but for most of their business and personal affairs they can find what they're looking for on their local-area network.

If the connection to the outside world over cables or satellite transmission fails, the local-area network remains a secure, failsafe, hardwired utility.

With a private bulletin-board site, shareholders can keep it local by hiring fellow members for professional services. With localized social media, members can stay in touch and share their interests while bypassing the hassles and distractions infesting mainstream and global social media. With less nonsense and fewer distractions, members can more easily break out of their trance and emancipate themselves from their screens to meet up in person.

A good local-area network should host a matchmaker site to keep locals and guests informed about every possible event they might want to attend or person they would be interested in meeting. Everyone who wants to participate opens an account where they post what they are looking for along with their education, work history, skills, interests, favorites, current obsessions and long-term goals. The matchmaker gives both predictable and surprising advice. Matchmaker might guide you to a strange event that will open your mind to a new horizon. If a visiting professor is giving a lecture, everyone who might be interested in attending will be notified. Matchmaker might recommend a film showing at the Commonwealth Multiplex. If someone is planning a trip to France, they can make contact with all the people who've been there in the last few years. Let's say someone has a newfound fascination with Celtic mythology. They can seek out the most knowledgeable person in the field while contacting other people who share their curiosity.

Visitors logging on to the L.A.N. from public computers can join the fun by entering their interests in a matchmaker account to see if anything they failed to discover in their preliminary search comes up. So if a visitor arriving at the Welcome Center went to the same high school as a member, that member will be notified and a meet up arranged. And finally, lonely hearts can use matchmaker to get a date. Why post your personal info for all the world to see when you're just looking to meet someone who lives close by or happens to be visiting? Matchmaker will find your best local romantic matches free and easy.

In an open society, people should be able to get together for every conceivable reason. With properly equipped meeting facilities, anyone with an issue, an interest or a hobby can start a group. Even in the busiest of times, a multi-use meeting facility will likely have weekly, one hour evening timeslots available for start-up groups.

Once people stop using information against one another, trust will be restored, peace will prevail and the quest for harmony will be fulfilled. There will be no more fools and no more foolers. Common sense will at last be common. The wisdom of the ages will finally be in full use.

7.–Local Harmony

If you were a founding member of a successful private-commonwealth municipality—What exactly would you be enjoying after all the challenging work you poured your heart and soul into?

You will not be floating on clouds. No celestial choirs will fill the air with luscious harmonies and mesmerizing melodies. Your fellows will not be lounging about placid pools surrounded by Gardens of Paradise with scantily-clad nymphs slavishly attending to their needs. Sorry–! The aim was not to be as Gods—rather to be fully human. What you will have to enjoy is a safe, clean, modern city with plenty of interesting places to visit, loads of stuff to do and plenty of interesting people to meet. I hope that's good enough for you.

Picture yourself walking through a newly completed city of the future. On the surface it might not appear very different from other modern cities. People going about their business. A wallet in your pocket. Money in the bank. The usual concerns. As you reflect on the ordinariness of it all, you pause to wonder what the fuss was all about. Then a huge relief overcomes you as you begin to notice what's missing from the picture—all sorts of worries and hassles. You slowly realize there was so much nonsense you had become used to that you were barely conscious of it. Taking off the blinders, you're beginning to enjoy a fuller view. Your inner clarity increases as your mind steadily expels the brain garbage. You briefly miss all the hustlers and colorful characters hanging on your old street corner. Then you remember all the players who acted like they were on your side when they were really trying to take you for a ride. You recall all the loveable losers who were dragging you down. You kept on helping them and helping them and they never got their lives together. Then you recall all the abusers: the mean bosses, grumpy neighbors and spiteful co-workers you no longer have to deal with.

You think about all the friends you lost along the way who said you were crazy to pursue a wild dream. They chided you for wanting to live in *La La Land*. But you never let go of your ideals and it paid off. People who made fun of you now want to be one of you. You're on the inside while they're on the waiting list. They said it could never be done, but now people on both sides of the fence realize goodness can triumph. Your pretend-a-friends are gone and now you have real friends who really care.

You reflect on the mythological past you left behind: the myth of the rugged individual and the alpha male; the myth that just because it's been a certain way for so long, it always has to be that way; the myth that technology will be humankind's salvation. You think about all the worn-out clichés that no longer hold sway. Money is no longer the root of all evil because your society has the money game figured out. You know power doesn't always corrupt because your political system generates power without any cheaters spoiling the game by claiming more than their fair share. The nonexistence of the imperialistic mindset within your community grants true peace of mind. You no longer have to put up a defensive shield to protect yourself from the ceaseless efforts to invade, persuade, convince and influence you.

Imagine this: no one lives in isolation anymore. There are no mansions on the hill. There is no ghetto on the outskirts of town. Everyone you need to know is close by and before long you'll know where to find each and every one of them. It feels great to be part of something that has a future. It feels so right to participate in a way of living built on the wisdom of the ages rather than the whim of the moment. You'll feel free to speak your mind without fear of ridicule. You'll enjoy sharing your ideas because other creative people are receptive to your free thinking. You're no longer afraid to ask the difficult questions. How great to realize you are no longer living a life of hypocrisy. Your words match your deeds.

Locals are very aware of the Red Scare—the oldest propaganda trick in American political history, given its name in 1919. Fast forward 107 years and there's a New Red Scare, and sad to say the same old bag of tricks is working again on a new generation. Label anything as *collectivist, socialist, communalist*, God-forbid *communist* and many people expect nothing but foul play. Whatever label critics try to hang on a private-commonwealth municipality, the small non-profit (socialist) sector is built to enhance the large free-market (capitalist) enterprise system of hundreds of companies doing their best to earn a healthy profit and their darndest to invest their capital wisely over the coming years.

You marvel how there is so much to do in our big small city. It's big enough to feature a wide variety of entertainment and recreation, yet small enough to walk across in less than an hour. You look forward to doing a full tour of the marvelous Marketplace. Holy smokes—so much must have happened since your last visit. You're making plans for an extensive walk through the Industrial Park. You've been hearing the stories for long enough and now you have to see for yourself.

Well, guess what? It's happening. No need to talk about it anymore because love is happening. You feel the energy of goodness and the power of a culture of fairness. You were living in a world turned upside down and now you're living in a world turned right-side up.

End Notes

One morning in the early 2005, I was hitchhiking across Taos, New Mexico, where I was living at the time, and an old Volvo station wagon pulled over to give me a ride. The older gentleman behind the steering wheel introduced himself as Steven. He was friendly and unassuming. He asked me a lot of questions about Taos, so I knew he was from out of town. When he dropped me off and drove away, I noticed his car had Tennessee plates.

Later on I found out it was Stephen Gaskin, the inspired founder of The Farm in Summertown, Tennessee: the largest and longest lasting of the hippie communes. As I was in the final stages of editing this book, I came across a film on You Tube: *American Commune*. Watching the film helped me realize what an inspiration the Commune Movement must have been. I obviously fell in love with the romantic notion of buying a big rural property in the boonies and building a society from scratch.

I also came across a film *American Heretic*, which is about two Unitarian churches and two sets of heretics in Tulsa and Oklahoma City. This aroused my curiosity to visit a Unitarian church. First I visited the uptown church, on St. Charles Ave of all places. Then I visited the Lakeview church and found my college buddy was the music director. So... I'm back where I started long ago exploring churches.

Short Author Bio

I am a native New Yorker born in 1960. I grew up watching the Viet Nam War and Civil Rights Movement on television in the '60s and came of age in the '70s absorbing the great art and high idealism of that era. I attended the State University of New York in Binghamton for two years but failed to earn a degree. In the early 1980s, I worked for the Federal Reserve Bank for two years, then was a fashion entrepreneur for ten years, then a carpenter and construction tradesman for twenty years. I have lived in Florida, Colorado, New Mexico and briefly in California. My pressing questions about the state of the world and my personal frustrations inspired prolonged investigations of religion, history and philosophy. When I had the idea to write a book in the early '90s, I inadvertently started my writing career. I moved to New Orleans eighteen years ago, and in December, 2016, completed a bachelor's degree in history at the University of New Orleans.

Author Notes

My categorization of *Blueprint for Local Harmony: A People's Guide to Utopia* (in small print on the back cover) as "romantic philosophy" is, strange to say, rather accurate. Romance is the quest to live an extra-ordinary life, defy boundaries and change the world. A philosophy is an organized body of principles. This book presents an organized framework of ideas aimed at people yearning to live an extraordinary life. This book outlines a path to seek one's own happiness by way of improving the world. The goal of the book is to open the reader's imagination to visions of a better future. I want to convince readers that the world can be transformed by describing the nuts and bolts of the new world ahead.

Blueprint for Local Harmony is creative non-fiction of a particular sort: not a traditional scholarly book based on a formal research project. The book proves its arguments by simple common sense, not on suspicious social-science research, zany esoteric principles or outlandish claims.

This book is not based on the findings of a formal academic research project, nor is it the reflections on a long career in a particular profession. I am an unpublished writer who just kept plugging away at it despite many personal setbacks, set asides and fallow creative periods. I persisted in this grand project because I believe the solutions presented in this book are what many people are looking for and the plans presented in these pages can really get to the root of the problems plaguing modern society. This opus was inspired by my experiences struggling for success in a relatively unsuccessful life, and developed through my subsequent study of history, economics, philosophy and English.

I returned to school in the fall of 2012 to attend Delgado Community College in New Orleans. After four semesters at Delgado, I transferred to the University of New Orleans. After five semesters at U.N.O, in December 2016, I graduated with a B.A. in History with incomplete minors in Economics and English.

Most readers will be able to fully relate to what I express without an advanced education or a gigantic leap of faith. Readers don't have to take my word for anything because what I discuss is rather close at hand and of direct concern. One day I just started writing down my ideas and kept on going, so it is impossible to trace every idea to its original inspiration. I do my best to write in an informal, conversational style that clearly expresses a rather complicated set of ideas without interrupting the flow to acknowledge where each idea came from. This reference-free style of presentation leaves the text free of flowery quotations by thinkers most readers are unfamiliar with.

It is frustrating being a generalist. I am a jack of all trades and a master of one vocation of synthesizing a broad range of thought into a singular vision. There are no annual convocations of generalists and there is no way to specialize in general knowledge. Because I am expressing a call to action and calling this book a *guide*, I aimed to be as thorough as possible. I also recognized that the estate model / intentional village concept could be adopted independently from a larger amalgamation, so I went out of my way to flesh out a wide variety of adaptations of the estate model, especially rural estates.

I chose to self-publish because of the non-traditional nature of this book and my lack of social-media following. I have no platform to stand on. My lack of stature as a writer would give me little bargaining power with agents and publishers. The irony of my predicament is I don't particularly enjoy working alone. I would prefer being a team player. I am not trying to sneak past the gatekeepers. I would love to find a good agent and publisher.

I will not attempt to fully defend publishing a non-fiction book that does not have a comprehensive bibliography. I encourage readers to verify what I have to say and investigate any topic of interest. My only defense is I've done my best under the circumstances. I believe I have succeeded in communicating what I intended in an accessible and orderly manner. I would not mind mavens, enthusiasts, experts and scholars taking me to task concerning my treatment of specific topics. Just tell me what you disagree with and why.

www.ingramcontent.com/pod-product-compliance
Lightning Source LLC
Chambersburg PA
CBHW060409130626
46555CB00005B/2013